A SELF-DEVELOPMENT PROGRAMME

Working with difficult people

A SELF-DEVELOPMENT PROGRAMME

Working with difficult people

THE ESSENTIAL GUIDE TO THINKING AND WORKING SMARTER

Bobbi Linkemer

MARSHALL PUBLISHING • LONDON

A Marshall Edition
Conceived, edited and
designed by
Marshall Editions Ltd
The Orangery
161 New Bond Street
London W1Y 9PA

First published in the UK
in 1999 by
Marshall Publishing Ltd

Copyright © 1999
Marshall Editions
Developments Ltd

ISBN 1-84028-278-9

Series Consultant Editor
Chris Roebuck
Project Editor
Jo Wells
at Axis Design
Design
Siân Keogh
at Axis Design
Indexer
Theresa Reynolds
at Axis Design
Art Director
Dave Goodman
Managing Art Editor
Patrick Carpenter
Managing Editor
Clare Currie
Editorial Assistant
Dan Green
Editorial Coordinator
Becca Clunes
Production
Nikki Ingram

Cover photography
Tony Stone Images

Originated in Italy by
Articolor
Printed and bound by
Printer Portuguesa

Contents

Chapter 1

Who is difficult? 8

Why do people behave like that? 9

Personality types 12

Putting behaviour in boxes 13

Chapter 2

Remember, this isn't about you 16

Stay centred 17

Choose your response 18

Are you proactive or reactive? 19

Ask questions 20

Use assertive communication 22

Negotiate 24

Let them vent 25

Use conflict resolution
    techniques 26

Chapter 3

Don't allow yourself to be abused 30

Don't fight fire with fire 32

Don't be a hero 36

Don't be afraid of conflict 38

Don't get drawn in 42

Chapter 4

A plan for harmony 46

Be open-minded 47

Plan and set the scene 48

Confirm your understanding 50

Let the other person talk 52

Look for areas of agreement 54

State your position 55

Talk through problem areas 56

Resolve the issue 57

Follow through 58

Chapter 5

Maslow's pyramid 62

Getting the whole picture 65

Difficult bosses 66

Difficult peers 72

Difficult employees 74

In meetings 78

Case study: customizing the
    steps 80

Chapter 6

What are your options? 86

Accept and adjust 87

Change something 88

Leave 92

Conclusion 94

Index 95

1

The changing workplace
Personal problems
Different personality types
Managing yourself

Who is difficult?
Why do people behave like that?
What strategies can you use?

Who is difficult?

REASONS WHY PEOPLE CAN'T GET ALONG

- The accelerated pace of change
- Lack of good, old-fashioned manners
- Increased diversity in the workplace
- Boring jobs
- Stressful jobs
- Personal problems
- Cynicism

You can encounter "difficult people" just about anywhere you go. Remember, though, that difficult is often in the eye of the beholder; and, while you are applying that label to someone, he or she may be applying it to you. Assuming, however, that some people really are perverse, you could run into them on the bus or the train; in shops; on the phone or at your front door; in your home, your children's school, and even your place of worship.

In many cases – except perhaps at home – you have the option of beating a hasty retreat when the atmosphere becomes too unpleasant. But in the workplace, there is often no way out, no choice but to stay there and face it. The world of work is filled with people, each with a unique personality. If you are going to deal effectively with this vast array of people, you will need to be able to respond appropriately to each of their personalities.

Some people are easy to work with. You get along, you work well together, and you think of them as pleasant and congenial. Some people elicit no response at all. Finally, there those who can ruin your day in an instant. You find them disagreeable, abrasive, or totally non-communicative – in other words, "difficult."

A personal point of view

"Difficult" means "hard to deal with, manage, overcome, or understand." But labelling someone "difficult" is a subjective assessment. You might find a fellow worker hard to understand or difficult to deal with, but someone else might view the same person as cooperative and good natured.

You are both right, because each of you experiences this person based on your own unique perceptions, which are filtered through your senses and personal history. No two people perceive the world in the same way, so others may not share your opinion.

The truly difficult person

There are some people with whom few people can get along. If virtually everyone finds one member of the work group abrasive, abusive, uncooperative, unreasonable, or volatile, you can safely assume that this is truly a "difficult person."

Difficult people do exist. They do try our patience and puzzle us. There may be some reasons why someone at work is always difficult to deal with or why someone who is generally easy to deal with may become a thorn in your side. Often understanding the reasons for someone's behaviour gives us a better chance of dealing with them effectively.

Why do people behave like that?

There may be any number of reasons why someone's behaviour is difficult in the workplace. Sometimes, understanding what lies behind it can make it easier for you to cope. Here are some common factors.

Times of change

When people find themselves in constantly changing circumstances, they may have difficulty getting their bearings. What was once familiar is replaced by something totally new and unfamiliar, and old expertise no longer applies. People in unfamiliar territory, for example, confronted by technology or procedures they don't understand, are likely to become edgy and unpleasant to be around. It is the rare individual who thrives on change and eagerly embraces the unknown and untried. Most of us feel slightly off balance, inept and unsure of ourselves until we master each new machine, procedure, or skill. During such periods of transition, people may become more difficult to work with than normal.

A lack of manners?

It may seem that one of the most apparent changes in society is the disappearance of old-fashioned manners. It can sometimes seem that the most simple courtesy – phrases such as "please", "thank you" and "you're welcome" – are no longer part of everyone's vocabulary.

Unfortunately, this may be true of some of your co-workers. When almost every task is deemed urgent, past the deadline, or a mandate from management, courtesy is often the first casualty.

People are not born polite and well behaved; they learn these things – first at home, then at school or in their place of worship and finally from other role models. They learn by example, by being instructed on appropriate responses to situations and by being corrected when they are out of line.

In 1970, author and futurist Alvin Toffler coined the term "future shock" to describe a condition of distress and disorientation caused by the inability to cope with rapid change. Before the ink on his book was dry, much of what Toffler had written was already obsolete. There has been more change in the past 50 years than in the preceding 5,000.

THE ONWARD MARCH OF OFFICE TECHNOLOGY

The electric typewriter was a rather sophisticated piece of office equipment in its day. When cumbersome word-processing machines came along, many secretaries found them intimidating, hard to learn and a potential threat to their jobs.

Personal computers have invaded and transformed the workplace, and have become another cause of uncertainty. Most office professionals did master them and soon became quite proficient, but many managers and executives balked at having to keep track of their own schedules, answer e-mail and learn to type.

Why do people behave like that?

Increased diversity in the workplace

If you look around the workplace there is a growing variety of people, partly due to increased mobility around the world, partly due to increased opportunities for everyone. Diversity is a fact of life in today's business world. You are likely to be working with a mixture of people, older and younger people, people of a different sex, country of origin and culture, and some with disabilities.

The unknown can be unsettling, especially if there are language barriers, differences in work styles, or even personal styles.

Stereotyping and prejudice are unfortunate realities. Some people fear what they don't understand or find "different" from themselves. These feelings can create fertile ground for uninformed judgments, rudeness, and bigotry. In such cases, "difficult" becomes an understatement.

Boring jobs, stressful jobs

It has been said that the mass of men lead lives of quiet desperation. Nothing produces such a state of mind faster than a go-nowhere, repetitive, unstimulating job, especially if the job holder is overqualified for the work. Such thoughts as, "Every day, the same old thing… I deserve better than this…

No one ever says 'thank you' or 'good job'… I might as well be invisible for all the recognition I get", are not only common, they are often justified. People who feel unimportant, undervalued, and unappreciated are not likely to have the cheeriest dispositions. Consideration for others and proper workplace decorum are rarely in evidence when workers feel they are wasting the best hours and days of their lives.

The opposite of boring is stressful. In one case, the hours drag; in the other, they fly by. There is never enough time to do what must be done. Impossible deadlines, other people's priorities, responsibility without authority, doing more with less, doubling up on work because laid-off co-workers are not replaced, militaristic management style, lack of communication or direction, and scores of other stress-producing policies exhaust the average person's psyche, as well as his or her adrenal glands. One can only call upon the flight-or-fight response so many times before it simply stops responding.

Stress is a killer. There is so much evidence to support that statement that no one bothers to dispute it anymore. There is not a single serious illness that is not linked to stress, from the common cold to cancer. When people are pushed too hard and stretched too far, their whole organism reacts – usually by breaking down physically or mentally. They get sick; they get depressed; they get careless; they get cranky; they get "difficult".

Personal problems outside work

Life is not neatly divided into compartments with the contents of each isolated from the others. We take our work home and our home life to work. Problems outside of the workplace are often the culprits that explain difficult behaviour at work. People face myriad personal problems, and these are reflected in their personalities and interpersonal relationships. Personal problems preoccupy the mind, hamper concentration, decrease productivity, and most certainly play havoc with workplace relationships.

Cynicism

Once upon a time employers and employees had an understanding – an unwritten, informal contract that promised employers loyalty and hard work from their workers in return for job security and protection. Organizations were paternalistic, often treating their employees like children, telling them

what to do and how to do it, and "taking care of them" during the tough times. Employees repaid this by giving 100 percent of their effort and staying with the company until they retired.

Times have changed. That informal contract is in shreds. People are willing and able to change jobs much more frequently; and companies also regularly change their workforce through mergers, acquisitions, bankruptcies, downsizing, and lay-offs. As a result, a creeping cynicism seems to be infecting much of the working population.

Cynics are closed minded and disillusioned. They see the worst side of every situation and every person. They believe that other people are self-centred and self-serving. Cynicism can be caused by a lack of security and a purely financial relationship at work; a lack of meaningful, challenging work; limited opportunities for advancement; and destructive management styles.

Cynics are rarely upbeat, happy, team players. They tend to have an expression that communicates, "Oh, yeah? Prove it to me." This attitude is naturally reflected in their day-to-day behaviour, particularly at work. While cynics see the world as "difficult", that is how their fellow workers see them.

PERPLEXING BEHAVIOUR MAY BE DUE TO:

- a bad day
- illness
- personality type
- a bad performance appraisal
- depression
- problems at home
- being passed over for a promotion
- divorce

Personality types

People respond to identical situations in their own unique ways. While one person may get angry and storm off, another will stand her ground and fight. The same event can elicit responses as varied as tears, laughter, a temper tantrum, silence or sarcasm. People might act one way today and differently tomorrow. But there are always reasons why.

Behaviour models

The desire to understand behaviour has led to the development of models – attempts to categorize various types of behaviour. The theory is that if you know what makes others tick, you can adapt your behaviour to theirs.

Each model approaches behaviour from a slightly different perspective. For example, one is based on cognitive style – the way people think and approach problems. Another model measures your orientation to tasks and people on a scale from 1 to 9. The higher the number in each of these categories, the more attention you tend to give either tasks or people. A 9,9 score for example, indicates high concern for both tasks and people – the sign of a good leader. A score of 1,1, on the other hand, clearly points to a lack of leadership ability.

The important thing to remember is that the models apply to behaviour, not people. It's a subtle distinction but an important one. By labelling people instead of their behaviour, we put them in boxes, a way of thinking that is potentially destructive to healthy working relationships and encourages stereotyping.

THE MYERS-BRIGGS TYPE INDICATOR (MBTI)

One of the best known models, called the Myers-Briggs Type Indicator (MBTI), classifies behaviour into four main types, which can be combined in 16 different ways. The four types are designated by the letters I, N, F and J, standing for Introvert, iNtuitive, Feeling, and Judging. When scores for these different behavioural characteristics are plotted on a graph, what emerges is a four-letter profile that sums up a person's dominant behaviour patterns.

- **INTROVERSION** means you relate more easily to the inner world of ideas than to the world of people and things.
- **INTUITION** indicates that you would rather look for possibilities and relationships than work with known facts.
- **FEELING** suggests a preference for basing judgments on personal values rather than analysis and logic.
- **JUDGING** means you are more attracted to a planned, orderly way of life than to a flexible, spontaneous style.

Putting behaviour in boxes

One behavoural model divides behaviour into four categories, based on dominant or passive tendencies and concern for people or lack of it. If your behaviour matches one of these rather exaggerated descriptions you may behave in some of the following ways.

PROACTIVE (CONTROLLING) + NO CONCERN FOR PEOPLE

Proactive, controlling, and lacking in concern for people, you feel a need to take charge, run the show, grab the credit, and take all the bows. You have little faith in or concern for others. Whatever it takes to get your way, that's what you'll do. You're likely to lose your temper and sometimes use anger as a club.

PROACTIVE (DECISIVE) + PEOPLE ORIENTED

Proactive, decisive, and people oriented, you are willing to lead the charge, make tough decisions, share the spotlight, and control the situation but not the people in it. You listen to input and suggestions, but ultimately do what you feel has to be done. You will not undermine or run roughshod over people.

REACTIVE (PASSIVE) + NO CONCERN FOR PEOPLE

Reactive or passive, and with little regard or trust for others, you tend to shun responsibility, avoid the spotlight, keep your thoughts and feelings to yourself, take whatever anyone dishes out, even if you don't like it and fume inwardly. You are apt to sulk or pout rather than confront the issue or the offending person.

REACTIVE (INDECISIVE) + PEOPLE ORIENTED

Reactive and indecisive, but warm and friendly, you don't like to make decisions, get people angry, be a leader or a star. You like to be a team player, to be well liked, and to let your co-workers, subordinates or boss bask in the spotlight and take the credit. While you don't get angry, you do get easily hurt.

Have you ever been baffled by someone's behaviour? Perhaps you have wondered:

- What was that all about?
- What did I do to her to make her so mad?
- What's wrong with the boss today?
- Why did my co-worker just snap at me?
- How can the person who delivers the mail be so unfailingly cheerful?
- Why doesn't the man down the hall ever talk to anyone?
- Why doesn't the person at the next desk ever stop talking?

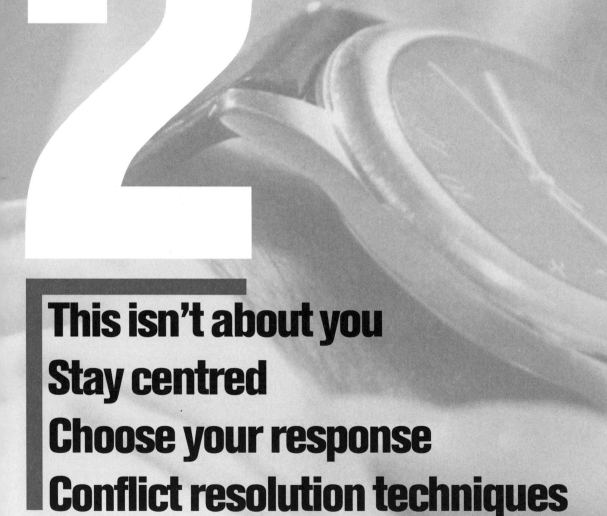

2

This isn't about you
Stay centred
Choose your response
Conflict resolution techniques

How can I take control?
What should I say?
Can questions help?

Remember, this isn't about you

POSITIVE SELF-TALK IN A DIFFICULT SITUATION

"This isn't about me."

"I can stay calm."

"We can resolve this."

The most valuable thing you can do when dealing with a difficult person is to remember who owns the problem and that it is not you. Whatever is going on, you can almost always say, "This isn't about me," and be sure you are correct. Remember that sentence and make it your mantra, especially during arguments, put-downs and other uncomfortable situations precipitated by someone else. While this is a powerful and very effective piece of advice, it is also the most difficult to follow.

A stressful scenario

Imagine your boss is angry. She is yelling at you. She is blaming you for something she says caused her a problem. Her behaviour is intimidating, abusive and embarrassing. You are caught off guard and feel the familiar flight-or-fight response. This is your boss, so fighting is risky. Fleeing, on the other hand, is possible – if not by physically turning on your heel and walking away, at least by shutting down and disengaging from the situation.

You may think that it must be your fault that your boss is in this state, that you are in the wrong. But it's *not* your fault. Pull out your new mantra. Remember, this isn't about you; it's about your boss. Even if, in the end, it turns out that you did cause her a problem, the response, the anger and the harsh words are hers. While she is making you the source and recipient of the problem, it remains her problem, not yours.

What lies behind it?

There may be any number of reasons, besides this issue, why she is flying off the handle, perhaps not even related to work. Your boss may have brought a personal problem to work today, and that might well be what is fuelling her outburst. You can't know what is happening in the background of her mind. She may not even know.

Anger is a choice

Even if you are guilty of whatever infraction has set her off, is anger the only possible response to what you did? Hardly. Someone else might brush it off without a word. A different boss (or your boss on a better day) might discuss it with you in a calm, reasonable manner. There are many ways your boss could have responded to this situation. But, *she chose* – consciously or not – to get angry. She missed or ignored the opportunity to stop, consider and decide how to react. No matter how you look at this, it simply is not about you; it's about her!

Stay centred

To be centred means to be stable, steady, grounded – to exercise self-control, self-restraint, self-mastery, and self-possession. It implies that you have an unshakable inner core, that you know who you are, and that you don't change every time the wind blows or life hands you a set of circumstances you don't particularly like. That may sound a bit abstract, but it is a very valuable concept.

People often forget their central core. In the face of trouble and turmoil we may lose our sense of self and sometimes allow ourselves to behave in a way that is completely contrary to who we are.

Losing your centre

Imagine this scenario – you like your co-workers, and they seem to like you. No one thinks of you as "difficult." You certainly don't think of yourself that way. But one day you find yourself in a contentious discussion with someone from another department. No matter what you say or how you say it, this person doesn't seem to hear you. Instead of a dialogue, you find yourself engaged in sequential monologues: first one of you talks and then the other, but there is no connection between what the two of you are saying. When you try to respond, the other person veers off in another direction. The tone is getting sharper; the decibel level is rising; and your level of annoyance is rising right along with it. Suddenly you hear yourself shouting.

It's true the other person shouted first, but you are definitely shouting back. You are stunned. "Who is this person?", you ask yourself. "What's happening here?" What's happening is that you have lost your centre. You've been thrown off course and on some level forgotten who you are deep inside. You found yourself in an escalating situation of miscommunication and frustration. Like a tree in a storm, you felt blown all over the place; but, unlike the tree, you fought the storm.

You could have stepped back and simply observed the storm as it began to gather momentum. You could have become a witness to, rather than a participant in, the argument. You could have reminded yourself of things you know – that you are rational, smart, flexible, diligent, well liked, and open-minded. You could have refused to continue this fruitless discussion and suggested a new start or a break. In all of these actions you would have remained true to who you are – certainly not a person who resorts to shouting in order to be heard.

BE LIKE A TREE
A tree is one of the best examples of being centred. Seasons come and go, wind makes it sway and bend, sun warms it, ice weighs down its branches; but, through it all, the tree keeps standing, taking each thing as it comes and remaining true to itself. Throughout all this activity, it is busy taking in nourishment, sprouting leaves and growing.

Choose your response

There are two ways to respond to any situation: one is reactive; the other is proactive. What that means is that when something occurs, you will have either a spontaneous, knee-jerk reaction to the event; or you will take a split second to decide exactly what you want to do. In the first, you are being acted upon; in the second you are initiating the action.

Being proactive is closely linked to centredness. When you know who you are and what you are about, you are less likely to be thrown off balance by someone or something that is outside your control.

Reactive people live from the outside in. They are affected by the weather, the attitudes and behaviour of others, and the endless stimuli thrown at them by life. Proactive people live from the inside out, choosing their own responses to life. It is not an exaggeration to say that you can always choose the way you will respond to situation. There are countless examples of people who have done it in seemingly impossible situations.

An inspirational story

Proof of this statement can be found in a book called *Man's Search for Meaning*, written by Victor Frankl. The book is a classic that has influenced and inspired millions of people over the years. Victor Frankl was a German-Jewish psychiatrist, interned in a Nazi death camp during World War II. Almost every member of his family died in that camp, and he never knew from one day to the next if he would survive. He watched others undergo torture, deprivation, and death. He experienced all the suffering and degradation to which any human being could be subjected. Yet he prevailed.

With nothing left – no dignity, no hope of survival, no reason to go on – Frankl called upon what he would later call "the last of the human freedoms" – the right to decide for himself how he would respond to his circumstances. He took responsibility for his own behaviour, determining it by his own decisions, not by outside conditions. If he could do it in a concentration camp, surely we can do it in the workplace.

Are you proactive or reactive?

Read each statement, and score yourself according to how often you behave in the same way in similar situations: always, frequently, sometimes, rarely or never? Then add up your total and read your assessment.

Statement

When my boss criticizes me publicly, I listen calmly and ask if we might continue the discussion privately.

When I am in the middle of a task and a co-worker drops by to chat, I explain that I am busy and suggest we talk later.

When I am overwhelmed with work and my manager gives me another assignment, I ask for help in prioritizing my workload.

If I have difficulty getting information from a co-worker, I point out the benefits of complying with my request.

When I am chairing a meeting and someone introduces an irrelevant topic, I quickly get the discussion back on track.

When one of my peers is uncharacteristically snappy, I look for clues to the problem or ask tactfully if something is wrong.

When I am having a bad day I take care to think before I speak.

If fellow workers are arguing I remain uninvolved.

When someone is displaying great emotion, I acknowledge their feelings but do not judge whether they are justified.

When I find myself getting angry or defensive, I admit my feelings and say that I need time to think through the issue.

Scoring Method

1 = never
2 = rarely
3 = sometimes
4 = frequently
5 = always

How did you score?

41–50

You are usually successful at thinking before you react and taking responsibility for your responses and behaviour. The trick is to make it a habit.

21–40

Sometimes you respond rather than react; other times you act before you think. Use the advice in this chapter to increase your proactive responses.

10–20

You tend to shoot from the hip, reacting first, thinking later. Try counting to ten, deciding what is the best thing to do, and calmly doing it. This will take self-discipline until it feels natural to you.

Ask questions

If there is one skill you cannot do without when working with difficult people, it is the art of asking the right questions. Questions are powerful and people respond better to questions than to statements. If you tell someone something, they may ignore you; but if you ask a question, they will immediately perk up. People love to talk – about their feelings, their opinions, their ideas and themselves. A question may unleash a torrent of words, but it will give you time to centre yourself and choose your response. Asking questions will also provide you with information to help you deal effectively with the situation and person.

Persuasion

Questions may help you to persuade someone to do something. Let's say you have a new process in mind that you know will work. If you suggest it to your boss, she may be unenthusiastic, but if you ask a question like, "How do you think this could improve our overall efficiency?" or "Do you have some ideas on how we could persuade the director of its value?" you may find that she will not only love the idea, she may even take credit for it later.

Understanding

Questions, or statements that are questions in disguise, demonstrate your interest and help you understand the message and the meaning behind it.

For the message, you feed back the content of what you heard: "As I understand your response to this idea, you don't think it will work for our group and you'd like to hear some other suggestions. Is that correct?"

For the meaning behind the message, feed back the feelings, emotions, and nonverbal clues you have picked up and check that you have

THE POWER OF QUESTIONS
Questions accomplish amazing things. They can help you:

- persuade someone to do something you want done
- understand the message and the meaning behind the message
- verify your understanding of what you heard, saw, or sensed
- demonstrate your interest and concern
- open the lines of communication
- plant your ideas in a person's mind
- motivate people
- clarify instructions
- solve problems
- reduce anxiety
- overcome objections
- prevent and decrease errors
- defuse a volatile situation
- clear up fuzzy thinking - yours and theirs
- take the sting out of criticism
- put you in control of virtually any situation

interpreted correctly: "I can tell you're not happy about this. In fact, you seem quite upset. Am I right?"

Questions can help to clarify instructions, verify what you've heard, prevent errors and clear up misunderstandings. If you are given an assignment, you might ask, "Can I repeat this back to you to be sure I have it right?" If you are giving the assignment you could ask, "Can you tell me in your own words how you interpret these instructions?"

Calming a situation

Questions can help to defuse a volatile situation by getting the facts out on the table and by giving everyone involved a chance to express their feelings.

When someone is upset or angry it doesn't help to say, "Come on, cool down. Let's not make a big deal out of this." The other person probably thinks it is a big deal. On the other hand, asking a question like, "I can tell you're upset about this. Can you tell me why?" or "Do you want to talk about it?" or "Is there something I can do to help?" gives the other person a chance to put their case or to get something that is bothering them off their chest. By asking the question you have shown that you are interested and will listen to what they have to say.

ADVICE FROM A PROFESSIONAL

How you ask questions is just as important as what you ask. Here is some advice from an office manager in a large real-estate development office.

"Let's say a project is not getting done, and it's going to be late. The word-processing person working on it is already dissolving from fear, unravelling before my eyes. She knows I'm going to talk to her. She's upset in advance. If I want to find out what's going wrong here, I have to be very careful about what kind of questions I ask. And before I ask any, I have to set the stage. That means taking her aside somewhere quiet, where there are no interruptions, showing my concern for her, and empathizing with her feelings. I try to use this guideline – Where are we now? Where do we need to be? How are we going to get there? What do you need to do? How can I help you? – so that when we're finished, we have a plan. This is not the time for assigning blame; this is the time for getting the project completed."

Criticism

It is hard to take criticism, no matter how it's offered. You run the risk of putting the other person on the defensive or hurting their feelings. But if you ask, "How do you think you might improve your approach to this job next time?" it many not feel so much like criticism. If you've given an assignment and the deadline has passed, try this: "It looks like your plate is pretty full. What are your top priorities, and what would help you get them completed in time?"

Use assertive communication

A FASHIONABLE IDEA

Assertiveness as a communication skill has come in and out of fashion many times over the years. First it was hailed as the key to women's success in climbing the corporate ladder; then it was derided for making women too outspoken and pushy. Neither is true. What is true is that assertiveness is an equal opportunity skill – not a gender-specific one – and it is a very effective way to deal with any difficult person or situation.

Acting assertively is a way of making sure that your point of view is heard and that your needs and wants are met, without riding roughshod over others.

Behaving assertively has three key components.

- The first is standing up for your own rights and expressing what you believe, feel and want.
- The second is doing that directly, honestly and appropriately.
- The third is respecting the rights of the other person while you are doing it.

Get what you deserve

For most people this is a new way of communicating. We have been taught all through our school and business lives to express ourselves with caution, to carefully package what we say, and to be aware of the consequences of candour and directness.

And yet, ask yourself how many times you have walked away from a situation without getting what you deserved – like the rise or promotion you expected but didn't receive, or decent, courteous service from a sales clerk, or perhaps to be treated like an adult by your supervisor, instead of being patronized. How did you feel? Probably frustrated at the very least, and possibly downright resentful.

After all, you deserve to be fairly compensated and rewarded for good work; you deserve courteous service; and you deserve to be treated with respect. When you learn the art of assertive communication, you stand a much better chance of getting what you deserve. An additional benefit is that when you ask for what you want or express your feelings without apology or embarrassment and without attacking others in the process, your relationships will improve.

If you are a supervisor or manager, assertiveness will improve your effectiveness in making assignments, giving criticism or conducting performance appraisals. What's more, your employees will probably be more receptive to what you have to say and more willing to act on it.

Passive responses

One of the ways in which people tend to react to uncomfortable situations is to behave passively. But always avoiding confrontation has its price. If you abdicate responsibility for verbalizing your needs or guarding your rights, you ignore your feelings and lose control of the situation. No matter what the outcome, you lose – if nothing else, your self-respect.

Aggressive behaviour

You take the offensive, keep the upper hand, and get your point across but at a cost – the other person's feelings and rights. You may stand your ground and even get your way, but in the end you lose again – the other person's respect and possibly the relationship.

Which way would you respond?

Robert has a reputation for not being able to finish a task without help. He finds it easier to ask a co-worker to help him or to do it for him. Today, he needs information to complete a report. Here are three possible responses.

■ Passively?

I'm trying to finish my own report, which is due today. I'm really swamped, but if you're stuck, I suppose I could take a few minutes to give you a hand.

GUIDELINES FOR ASSERTIVENESS

- Express your feelings without trampling all over the other person's.
- Say "no" in a way that doesn't put either of you down.
- Seek the other person's understanding and acceptance of your position.
- Be direct; be appropriate; show respect for yourself and the other person.
- Pick the right time to say what's on your mind.
- Monitor the intensity of how you say it.
- Know the relationship you're dealing with.
- Repeat yourself when necessary.
- Let your body language do some of the talking.
- Let the other person respond.

■ Aggressively?

Look, Robert, all you have to do is log on to the company's web site, click the mouse a couple of times, and what do you know? Information!

■ Assertively?

I can see that you're having some trouble with this report, Robert, and I'd like to help you; but I can't do it today. I'm tied up with a project of my own for the next few hours. However, I think you might find the information you need on the company web site. It's loaded with up-to-the-minute data. Why don't you give that a try?

"Give straightforward business-like instructions"

Negotiate

Negotiation is the process of discussing a topic with the intention of arriving at an agreement that meets both parties' needs. In negotiating, neither side is supposed to exercise the power of position, even if one person has such power; neither side is supposed to bulldoze or manipulate; and neither side is expected just to cave in to the other person's demands. Presumably, a negotiation is a meeting of equals who come together to work through issues until they reach consensus.

Developing negotiation skills

The ability to negotiate is one of the most valuable skills you can cultivate. It will have a tremendous impact on your ability to get what you want, in the business world and in your private life. It will help you meet your needs and get ahead without riding roughshod over other people. It will make you a better manager; a better employee; and, in many ways, a better person. It will definitely help you work through issues with those whom you think of as "difficult people". And in the end it will make those people less difficult.

Discovering the other person's needs

Finding out what the other person wants and needs is the foundation of effective negotiations. Even if that person doesn't believe you are honourable in your intentions and fair in your methods, or if the conditions under which you are negotiating are not conducive to collaboration and trust, if you sincerely attempt to discover what that person needs and make a genuine attempt to provide it, barriers will begin to crumble.

PRINCIPLES THAT APPLY TO ALL NEGOTIATING SITUATIONS

■ Plan your negotiation strategies

■ Have high aspirations

■ Think win:win and mean it

■ Get your message across in understandable language

■ Have a spirit of inquiry, establishing genuine relationships

■ Maintain your integrity

■ Do not just give everything away

■ Hang in there for as long as the process requires

Let them vent

One of the things you can be sure of when you are in a difficult situation trying to deal with a difficult person is that there will be plenty of emotion flying around. You would probably prefer to avoid displays of uncontrolled emotion. After all, it's disturbing, embarrassing, and draining. But this is one time when it is essential that you deal with it, no matter how you feel.

If you are to get anywhere, you must get it out in the open and shine a light on it. That emotion will be like a brick wall between you and any kind of effective communication. The only way around that wall is to dismantle it, piece by piece using a process called "venting."

When someone is full of churning emotions, reasonable discussion is not possible. In fact, he or she is more like a pressure cooker ready to blow its top. Venting is a way of releasing that steam safely, rather than explosively. Once it is released it will dissipate and make discussion possible and even fruitful.

You can help a person who is experiencing great emotion to release that emotion by something as simple as acknowledging his or her feelings, which are usually pretty apparent. By simply observing, "You really seem upset," or "I can tell this is bothering you," you permit the other person to express, rather than hold back, those feelings. This is what venting is about.

Why is venting necessary?

If people just said what was on their minds, we wouldn't have to let them vent. There are many reasons why emotions get bottled up and remain unspoken. Venting helps us get in touch with and express those feelings in a safe and supportive environment.

WHY DO FEELINGS GET SUPPRESSED?

1 We have been socially conditioned to keep our feelings to ourselves, particularly angry feelings. We have learned to control outward expressions of what is going on inside.

2 Telling it like it is, especially when it is negative, can be risky. It may be safe to let your subordinate know when and why you're upset, but it is much less so to be as direct with your boss.

3 Some of us really have no idea what we are feeling. We are so out of touch that if we are confronted with a statement like, "I don't know why you're so angry about this," we may sincerely respond, "Angry? Who's angry? Not me. I have no idea what you're talking about!"

4 It is just plain uncomfortable for many of us to get angry and say angry things. Some people don't like to rock the boat or draw attention to themselves. Preferring to maintain the status quo, they may swallow words and feelings that might disturb it.

Use conflict resolution techniques

PAIN AND GAIN
The two things that get through to people are pain and gain. Pain is when your boss says, "You two need to work out a way to get along and work together in this department, or I am going to fire you both." Gain could be a promotion or anything considered a perk. The pain or gain has to be strong enough to influence the other person's emotional position.

Conflict resolution is often considered the realm of significant adversaries, such as union and management or participants in a divorce or custody battle. But its techniques are equally applicable to altercations between any two people, anywhere, particularly in the workplace.

It may take some time and persuasion to convince the other person to engage in this process.

The mediator

One of the key components of conflict resolution is the presence of a facilitator or mediator. It is that person's job to find a point of agreement that will get the parties to agree to talk. Sometimes it takes a while to find a real common point on which both sides can agree, but a well-trained mediator can certainly speed up this awkward process.

The venue

Provide a safe space in which to conduct the negotiation. Remove as many of the physical obstacles as possible so that neither side feels it is starting from a lesser position.

Venting

Give each side an opportunity to vent – to get its story on the table – without causing a greater rift between the two sides. Normally, the venting process takes place separately, with the mediator allowing each side to get the poison out. Once both sides have exhausted that venom, they come back together.

Find the common ground

Find one point to which both sides can relate. Sometimes this seems impossible, but there is always one thing that people share. There is a story of a very heated negotiation between two national leaders, in which the mediator felt unable to find a way to help them see each other as trusted individuals. They had 200 years of history, animosity and labels in the room with then. Finally, quite by accident, the mediator came upon a common denominator. Both of these leaders were males, and both were married. Both were having similar difficulties with their wives and their married children. When they began to see each other as husbands and fathers with similar problems, they could talk. The mediator used that common ground to melt their antagonism.

Feedback

Ensure that both sides feel they are being heard. Each point should be laid out and fed back, so that each person

BASIC GUIDELINES FOR SUCCESSFUL CONFLICT RESOLUTION

■ a safe environment
■ a belief that each side has been heard
■ common objectives
■ feedback

said everything there is to be said. In fact, you've probably said it several times. In the heat of battle, people tend to repeat themselves, thinking, for some reason, that repetition make things clearer. It doesn't. In fact, eventually people either tune each other out or shout, "Stop! You've already made that point – about ten times."

You take the lead by describing your present position. "We've been over this ground a number of times, and we don't seem to be making much progress. Both of us seem pretty committed to our own views, and I think we've gone as far as we can go today. I'd like to suggest that we take a break, give ourselves some time to think over what's been said here and come back fresh in the morning. How do you feel about that?"

has a chance to say, "This is what I heard," or "No, that's not what I said," or "Well, that's close. Let me say it a different way." That process takes place back and forth, back and forth, until all of the positions have been stated.

The feedback loop is important to ensure that, as each agreement is reached, everyone has the same understanding of what it is. You and the other person should be able to clearly state it so that both of you agree on the wording. The next step is to work out a plan and then repeat the feedback step to assure mutual understanding and commitment.

The key here is to keep your remarks focused on the process, not on the person. Be reasonable and calm. And ask for agreement on your suggestion. With time to think things over, tomorrow may find both of you in a more flexible frame of mind.

This chapter has presented a number of strategies to try when dealing with a difficult person or situation in the workplace. The next chapter explains behaviours to avoid during conflict.

Call time out

Let's say nothing has worked. You're stymied, absolutely out of ideas. What's left? Try taking a break from this circular discussion that is getting you nowhere. By this time, both of you have

3

Avoid an escalating situation
Do not be intimidated
Handling conflict
Dealing with violence

Should I fight back?
Does there have to be a winner?
Can anyone else help me?

Don't allow yourself to be abused

HOW TO SURVIVE VERBAL ABUSE

■ Understand that emotions have to be released.

■ Know that the thing you think will work, probably won't.

■ Keep the other person talking; let them vent.

■ Help the other person get in touch with their angry feelings.

■ Don't take it personally.

When someone is angry we feel the unwritten pact to act in a civilized way has been broken, and all order has broken down. When you are confronted with an angry person, it's very easy to feel intimidated or injured, especially if that person is someone with authority. People say things in the heat of anger that can be very destructive.

That old saying, "Sticks and stones can break your bones, but words will never hurt you," is simply not true. Words can hurt, and often the pain lasts a very long time.

How do you weather the storm?

It is not always easy to take the best course of action in a heated confrontation or tense and emotional situation. The answers to the question of how to weather the storm of someone else's anger are not always easy to apply, but you will get nowhere if you do not try.

1 Understand that emotions have to be released. You can't just let them sit there and hope they will go away, because they won't.

2 The strategies you might think will work – such as reason, distraction, changing the subject – are relatively worthless. Reason doesn't diffuse emotion. In fact, it may make the situation worse. Distraction won't work either. Don't try to change the subject or cheer the other person up, either. All they feel is anger and if you do talk, they simply won't hear you.

3 Keep the other person talking and let her vent. Eventually, she will spend the energy that is fuelling the emotion. Only if she talks will she be able to release the venom. When someone is screaming at you or using abusive language or sarcastically putting you down, it is pretty difficult to remain calm, let alone focus on her emotion and her need to purge it.

What you would probably prefer is for her to shut up, of course; but stand your ground.

4 Help the other person get in touch with their angry feelings – something else you might prefer not to do. Surely this person knows that they are having angry feelings? But this is not necessarily the case. It is truly amazing how someone can stand in front of you, shouting, spewing forth a litany of expletives, and looking like they may have a stroke at any moment, yet not know they are angry. If you pointed it out they would deny it. "I am not angry,

and I can't imagine what would make you think I am. I am perfectly calm!" is what they really believe.

This lack of awareness of their own feelings is even more characteristic of the person who, while not overtly angry, is seething inside. Nonverbal clues give them away. Perhaps you are aware that they show their anger in subtle, covert ways, such as being uncooperative, argumentative, or withdrawn.

In either case, you must make such people aware of what they are feeling. It won't be easy because all of us have developed very clever ways of hiding disagreeable feelings from ourselves. However, when the anger is spent, you might mention that he or she really does seem calmer now.

5 Don't take it personally. Try to remember that this isn't about you. Most people, of course, know they are angry when they are having a fit. They may fear losing control, but the advantages of unleashing their anger seem to outweigh the downside.

Anger is a way of controlling others. Many angry bosses certainly know that and use it for just that purpose.

WHAT NOT TO SAY

The other person is obviously upset, perhaps even very angry. Whether you think the emotion is justified is irrelevant. It exists and the person experiencing it is in its grip. There are some fundamental Don'ts. Don't belittle, ridicule, insult, smirk, or laugh. Don't start sentences with the word "you". Don't add fuel to the fire. Don't say things like:

■ I don't know why you're so angry about this.

■ You should see how red your face is.

■ Don't you think you're blowing this all out of proportion?

■ You're going to burst a blood vessel if you keep this up!

■ There you go again, flying off the handle.

■ Now I know you're crazy.

If control is not the reason, there may be others. Is this person a tyrant, or an emotional roller coaster, with mood swings all over the place? Does she get fired up and turned on, only to plummet into despair or anger? Any of those factors could be fuelling the anger.

"Avoid undignified kowtowing"

Don't fight fire with fire

When we are attacked, we either attack back or run away. That's called the "fight or flight response" and, if you examine your own style, you can see which of these choices you usually make. Your angry boss or co-worker may be expecting one or the other but will be caught off guard if you do neither. If it is possible for you to observe the anger (it would probably be hard not to) and do nothing, you have a great advantage.

Accept the emotion

Difficult people probably don't plan to have tantrums and would stop if they could, but they can't. Emotions are not always controllable. You cannot simply tell someone to stop being angry, but you can accept without judgment the emotion as it is spewing forth.

Try it the next time you are on the receiving end of anger. Simply don't take a position on it. Instead try to think something like, "Oh, here comes another explosion," then calmly watch the other person's emotion play itself out. Don't label it good or bad; don't criticize the other person or defend yourself. Just take it in your stride.

Let's face it, that advice is hard to put into practice, especially when this is not the first such occurrence with this person. It's tough to resist fighting back. It may be tempting to let the other person have it with a well-turned and lethal phrase or two. If you feel that you have reached your absolute limit, you might indeed be tempted to cut this person down to size, but resist the temptation and don't do it.

Why not retaliate?

What would you accomplish by having your say – by belittling, embarrassing, or hurting someone who is already a pretty unhappy person? How do you know the other person is unhappy? Well, how many happy, self-confident people do you know who deserve to be labelled "difficult," who argue at the drop of a hat, and who seem to have an unlimited supply of venom? Probably not too many.

If you respond in kind, it will surely lower you a notch in the estimation of anyone within earshot; it will preclude ever patching up the relationship with your momentary adversary; and it will make you drown in regret later on. Is it worth all that?

Written down in black and white, the list of dos and don'ts may seem very obvious. But it is easy to find yourself thinking and acting or reacting inappropriately in the heat of the moment, when you feel attacked and under a great deal of pressure.

How Dos Become Don'ts

The list of what you shouldn't do during a disagreement or conflict is the reverse of the advice from the previous chapter.

THESE ARE DOS	FLIPPED, THEY BECOME DONT'S
Remember, this isn't about you.	Don't think "This is personal, my ego is on the line here."
Stay centred.	Don't take advantage of the adrenaline rush, thinking it will pull you through this.
Choose your response.	Don't shoot from the hip, thinking your first response is always the best response.
Ask questions.	Don't tell her how you feel, in an attempt to get your side out before she does.
Practice assertive communication.	Don't be aggressive, thinking it's the only thing that works.
Negotiate.	Don't dig in your heels.
Let him vent.	Don't cut him off when he gets emotional.
Use conflict resolution techniques.	Don't think of the conflict as a war, doing whatever it takes to win.
Call time out.	Don't try to keep going until the other person is worn down or gives up.

Don't fight fire with fire

Fight your ego

For many difficult people, a conflict is personal, and their egos or self-images are definitely at stake. Be honest. For a moment, didn't you feel that way? If you are angry, it isn't easy to remember that this isn't about you. It certainly feels like it is.

Control your fighting instinct

There's no doubt that the adrenaline rush – the result of the flight-or-fight response – will pull you through, but at a cost. If you're angry enough, you are much more likely to fight than flee. If you take this approach often, eventually you stand a good chance of exhausting your adrenal glands. Fighting back is likely to escalate the problem and makes positive resolution less likely.

Consider your response

Shooting from the hip is dangerous, unless you're out to kill or be killed, so to speak. Your first response is unlikely to be the one you would stick with if you had time to reconsider. That's why adults often tell children to count to ten when they are angry. This is good advice throughout life. Counting to ten gives you time to calm down and possibly put together a coherent thought.

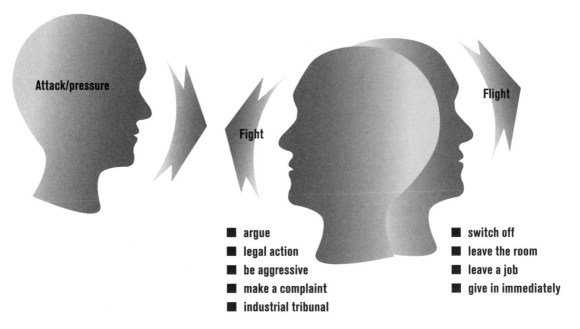

Attack/pressure

Fight

Flight

- argue
- legal action
- be aggressive
- make a complaint
- industrial tribunal

- switch off
- leave the room
- leave a job
- give in immediately

Listen first

If you tell your side of the story before the other person gets to tell theirs, chances are you'll never hear their side. You'll either drown them out, put them on the defensive, or trample on their arguments. Letting the other person have their say is one of the most important secrets of dealing with people – difficult or not.

Contain your aggression

Being aggressive is like shooting from the hip; it may backfire. In addition, it demonstrates no respect for the other person; it undermines your respect for yourself and others' respect for you; and it rarely works.

Acknowledge the emotions

If you don't let those emotions out in the open, where you both can deal with them, they will circle the room like a boomerang. They won't go away, and they won't permit any rational discussion to take place. Unexpressed emotions build an impenetrable wall between you – one that will make it even harder to cross the chasm your bad relationship has created.

Be prepared to compromise

Digging in your heels and standing your ground, no matter what, automatically makes a beneficial resolution impossible. It is a position that makes any discussion pointless and difficult. If you adopt this stance, although you may temporarily achieve what you want, the chances are that relations will deteriorate further and the same issue will resurface time and again. This is definitely not a war, and neither of you is going to emerge a winner. If you capitulate, the other person will say she won. If she capitulates, you could say the same thing. But you would both be wrong. If it got that far, both of you have lost. The only true resolution is one that you are both at least partly happy with. Aim for you both to win.

Call time out

If you do keep going until the other person wears out or gives up, you could be there forever; or you will wear out or give up first. Whoever gives up, the same issue will probably arise again at a later date; calling time out would have been a better idea.

Don't be a hero

While you are trying hard to keep your composure, bear in mind that, unless this person gets physical, you will be perfectly safe and the anger will dissipate. No one can rage forever.

Physical threat

However, there are situations in which people do lose control and become physically aggressive. When that happens, you are not perfectly safe; and this is no time to don your superhero costume.

The time to be proactive is before a situation escalates, not when it is already out of control.

Protect yourself

If you feel intimidated or at risk, here are some steps you can take to prevent a confrontation and protect yourself.

■ If there is time, call for help.

■ Alert your supervisor or the Human Resources Department about the situation and why you feel ill at ease.

■ Be aware of what you say and do in the presence of a threatening person; think about how he or she tends to respond to different situations.

■ Try to avoid being left alone with the person you feel threatened by.

■ Express understanding and empathy for this person's feelings.

■ Do nothing to exacerbate a potentially volatile situation.

■ If possible, quietly leave the premises.

WHAT TO DO IN A POTENTIALLY VIOLENT SITUATION

STAY AT LEAST TWO ARM LENGTHS AWAY
This allows you to avoid a possible punch. Back up slowly. If this person can't reach you, he can't hit you.

USE NATURAL OBSTACLES
Keep a desk or chair between you and the threatening co-worker. Move around so there is always something solid between you.

KEEP TALKING IN A CALM, NATURAL VOICE
Even berserk individuals seldom hit someone who is talking. They stop until the talking stops. Do not yell for help.

SOUND GENUINELY INTERESTED IN THE PERSON'S GRIEVANCE
Most rage is based on the feeling that one is not being listened to or taken seriously. When she tells you what she's feeling, repeat it in your own words to demonstrate understanding.

TELL THE PERSON IT IS NATURAL TO SAY THINGS ONE DOESN'T MEAN WHEN ONE IS UPSET
This will make it clear to that person that discharge or severe discipline due is avoidable if the confrontation ends immediately.

BUILD THE PERSON'S SELF-ESTEEM
Ego stroking is an excellent way to soothe raw nerves. For example, suggest that she is respected within the company and would be ruining a solid record because of a grievance that can easily be remedied.

POINT OUT WHAT YOUR COLLEAGUE OR BOSS CAN LOSE IF HE OR SHE GOES TOO FAR
Stress that the "too far" has not yet been reached; but, if necessary, security will be called. Point out that this situation can still be resolved peacefully and forgotten.

EMPATHIZE
This is not the time to disagree with the person's position, no matter how unreasonable it may be. Stress that you would feel the same way if you were in her shoes. Agree that the "beef" is legitimate but that there is a better way to resolve it.

NEVER THREATEN OR LOSE YOUR TEMPER
The worst thing you can do is retaliate in kind. Raising your voice or cursing can enrage him to the point where, if he has a weapon, he may use it.

Don't be afraid of conflict

Try asking yourself these questions when you're stymied by an adversarial relationship.

■ Does anyone have to be right or wrong?

■ Is this an ego problem?

■ Are you a space invader?

■ Is this argument even real?

■ Which should you believe: what you see or what you hear?

■ Is there anything you can agree on?

Conflict can range from an atmosphere of antagonism to outright animosity. Companies or departments characterized by conflict are always a little tense, a little on edge. Sometimes conflict is quite obvious, like anger. Other times it is disguised as friendly competition. But it is not friendly; and it takes its toll, especially if it simmers under the surface or goes on interminably. The ability to deal with conflict is a valuable survival skill; you never know when you may need it.

Find someone to talk to

Conflict in the workplace isn't always with a boss. It can take place between any two people or among any groups. It may or may not lead to overt anger, but that doesn't keep it from wearing you out, frazzling your nerves, and raising your stress level. Conflict is a normal part of life. You can't avoid it, so you have to learn how to resolve the situation and bring it to closure.

Sometimes it's difficult to do that, and you may need someone to talk to – a person you can trust to maintain confidentiality. This could be a friend, your boss, someone in Human Resources, or a counsellor at your company's employee assistance programme. But there is not always someone on hand to help you. Sometimes you may need to be your own best friend and the voice of reason.

Does there have to be a winner?

So often in arguments both sides fight with everything in them because they believe they have to be right. The implication is, if I am right, by definition, you must be wrong.

Of course, this point of view isn't true or even logical. For one thing, there is frequently more than one right answer, one right solution, or one right approach. There may be dozens. When you choose one over the others, it doesn't mean the others were wrong; it just means they were not right for you. If you see a situation one way and your boss sees it another way, you are merely coming from two different perspectives. The idea that there is no one right perspective cuts conflict off at the knees.

Is someone's ego on the line?

When tempers flare and the other person is getting passionate in their rhetoric, do you sometimes wonder if whatever you are arguing about is worth all this emotion? Ask yourself whether it is really an issue of life or death, or is it merely about control? Is one of you a personality type that always has to be a star, be in charge, be in control?

Could it be that this has nothing to do with the nuts and bolts of the topic under discussion and everything to do with personal needs – yours and your co-worker's? Does it matter to you who is in control or who gets credit? If it doesn't, just hand over the reins and end the conflict. It's that simple.

On the other hand, what if this argument really is about the nuts and bolts after all? If you and your peer are 180 degrees apart on an issue of substance and not of ego, what then? Then, you step back and seriously consider the other side. You might say, "If you feel this strongly about the subject, maybe I'm missing something here. Let me see if I can state the case you're trying to make, so I can see this from your point of view."

Is one of you a space invader?

Our sense of self isn't bounded by our skin. Most of us walk around inside a private, invisible bubble that represents the amount of airspace we feel we must have between ourselves and other people. The normal distance we tend to want between ourselves and co-workers is about 45cm (18 inches). If you invade that space, you trigger the other person's flight or fight response. That bubble is sacred space and is one of the unnoticed reasons for long-standing conflict in an office setting. You can easily observe this in an elevator. As each person gets out, everyone else unconsciously repositions themselves to make a little more private space. Another thing to be aware of is the person's cultural background, in which "space needs" may be different from yours.

What does this have to do with conflict? Now that you're aware of this need for personal space, observe what's going on when someone at work gets edgy and defensive for seemingly no reason. Are you getting too close? Step back, and observe that person's behaviour. If it eases up, you may have found an important clue.

Don't be afraid of conflict

Is this a real argument?

Sometimes what looks like conflict isn't that at all. It is merely what linguist and author Deborah Tannen refers to as "ritual opposition", a way of checking out the advantages and disadvantages of a particular idea. These discussions can get quite emotional, as questions and opinions are released in rapid succession. You or another member of the group may feel personally attacked, when actually it is just ideas that are under attack. The purpose of ritual opposition is to defend your ideas, not yourself.

If you feel defensive, try to re-focus on the content of the perceived attack, remind yourself that it is your ideas or point of view that are being questioned, not you as a person. If someone else seems to be getting too defensive, it may help to point out the dynamic that is actually taking place.

Should you trust what you see or what you hear?

The answer is what you see. Nonverbal and verbal messages often contradict each other. When that happens, what you see or sense is invariably more accurate than what you hear. When words and actions don't agree, the speaker is unaware of the discrepancy. As the saying goes, "Actions speak louder than words." If the words say, "I'm fine," and the body language says "I'm not fine," go with the body language. If you couldn't hear at all, you would depend on other senses to bring you information. Those who are deaf or hearing-impaired "listen" – often very effectively – through their senses of sight, taste, smell and touch, which are often much more accurate than words. Another way to "listen" is intuitively, and in this case trust your instincts and believe what you sense.

The whole truth? probably not

But don't get hung up on whether the verbal and nonverbal messages are the same or different and assume you are not getting the whole truth and nothing but the truth from your discussion partner. Chances are, even under the best of circumstances, you aren't anyway. Though we would all like to believe that we are honest to a fault and always tell it like it is, both notions are false. Few people are honest to a fault; and most of us hedge, package and edit what we say.

If you and your colleague have just had a knock-down, drag-out battle in order for you to get some information you want, and you finally get it, take it at face value. Assume it may be somewhat inaccurate or flawed, and accept it graciously. The worst thing you can do in a situation when you have achieved a small amount of progress is to then question the other person's honesty or the veracity of what they have said. If you do, it is unlikely that you will ever accomplish even such a partial victory again. The other person will probably think, "What's the point, you never believe me anyway."

Is there even one area of agreement?

One of the first rules of successful negotiation is to find one single area that both parties can relate to, and start from there.

It could be that you both have a personal interest in getting this project completed or that the team will benefit from your efforts. It may be something obvious or obscure. Sometimes it comes down to the fact that you are both of the same gender or age or ethnic background or stage of parenthood – all pretty personal areas – and one of those areas of common ground, even though it is unrelated to work, is sometimes all it takes to get the ball rolling. If you find one, take advantage of it.

The point is, if you are getting nowhere, arms folded across your chests, intractable, holding your ground, you could stay there for a long time. Who will this benefit? Surely not you, the other person, the department or the company. Seek out that one thing you can both agree on, and build on that. If this person is someone you know, the search for common ground may be easier than you think.

Don't get drawn in

One way to handle conflict is to purposely and consciously detach from the situation. When you are detached, you can examine what is being said or done objectively, try to figure out what's really going on and decide how you want to respond.

Whatever is happening around you, when you detach yourself from it, you will be able to act in a calm, sane manner.

Respond or react?

Responding is not the same as reacting. On one hand, reacting is emotional. It doesn't involve much thinking, which is probably why you may say something or do something you could regret later. On the other hand, responding is a planned action. You don't shoot from the hip. Instead you decide how you will handle this situation.

If the present situation is going to cause you to get angry, upset or out of control, detachment may not be enough. You may have to physically distance yourself.

There is no circumstance in which you don't have a right to leave. If you are in an angry confrontation with someone and it's getting out of hand, first, stay calm; and, second, if you must, leave. However, do not simply turn on your heel and walk away. Also, you cannot expect this course of action to resolve the issue once and for all.

How to leave

Some people are capable of knowing instinctively when and how to make an exit. Most of us, however, are not and we can feel trapped and panicked by a difficult situation. All you have to say is, "Excuse me. I think it would be better to continue this discussion at a later time." Then you simply walk away.

How you say you want to leave is important. When a person is angry and you speak in a soft, calm, even, measured manner, you not only diffuse the anger, you put yourself in control of the situation. If it is not your nature to respond this way, distancing yourself emotionally and physically is something you can teach yourself to do.

DETACH YOURSELF

Being detached means becoming separated or disconnected from the situation, standing apart from others. Detachment can be marked by an absence of emotional involvement and an aloof, impersonal objectivity. Detachment is not always easy to accomplish, especially in an adversarial environment. Becoming "separate" doesn't have to mean physically removing yourself; it may only involve emotional distance.

- Get your own emotions out of the way.
- Try to view the situation as an objective bystander would.
- Assume an attitude of "not caring" what is said or how it all works out.
- Stop listening, and think about something else.
- Appear to be disinterested or preoccupied.
- Change the subject.
- Excuse yourself and leave the room.

If you get it wrong

Even though you have every right to detach and leave, you may not always have the discipline to do so, especially if you have a hair-trigger temper. If you lose control and make the mistake of reacting, you can't undo what has already been done. But you can recover to some extent by admitting that you were wrong and apologizing.

You can say, "I was out of line. I was hurt and angry and I over-reacted. I am sorry." By doing so, you are taking responsibility for your own response.

Whether the other person admits they were wrong or accepts your apology isn't the issue. The aim of your apology is to try to remedy a bad situation, not to elicit an apology from the other person.

The next step

Now that you know what to do and not do, in a somewhat general way, let's get more specific. In the next chapter you will learn a ten-step formula for planning and implementing constructive interactions – even with the most difficult people.

4

The ten-step format
State your position
Talk through problems
Look for agreement

**Can you talk it through?
How can you resolve the difficulties?
Do you have common goals?**

A plan for harmony

When both parties are willing to have a discussion, that is a promising first step. While discussion may not necessarily lead to agreement, it will permit both people to air their views and to hear each other out. Dialogue leads the way to harmony.

Sometimes a problematic situation or relationship at work can be resolved simply by sitting down together and talking through the difficulty. If this is a possibility, the advantages of reaching a mutually beneficial agreement can transform your working environment and may even make the person who you once considered "difficult" one of your most valuable colleagues.

Getting the other person to agree to talk may not be easy, especially if that person is your boss. But once you have achieved this, no matter how difficult the other person, the situation, the relationship, or the work environment, there is a way to structure a discussion that will almost certainly lead to a positive outcome.

There is no guarantee that your point of view or argument will prevail, no matter how persuasive you are. With these steps, at least both parties will have their say and be heard, and the atmosphere will be civilized.

Ten-step format

1	Assume an open-minded attitude.
2	Prepare for the discussion.
3	Set the scene.
4	Confirm your understanding of the issue.
5	Let the other person talk.
6	Identify areas of agreement.
7	State your position.
8	Talk through areas of contention.
9	If possible, resolve the issue.
10	Follow through.

Be open-minded

Work towards a win:win situation. "Win:win" is an attitude, a way of ensuring that both you and the other person come out on top. What you are seeking is a mutually beneficial solution or agreement. When your discussion concludes, both of you should feel good about the outcome and be committed to the action plan you evolve. In a win:win situation, neither your way nor your adversary's way prevails. Together, you seek a better way. Compromise is a weak version of win:win, but it's better than some other less desirable outcomes.

This is not an attitude many of us are accustomed to in a business atmosphere. In a win:win situation, both of you get your needs met. Nobody loses. In the win:lose environment you may be accustomed to, this attitude requires a real shift in the way you look at the world.

Try to see the situation from the other person's perspective

One of the most important habits you can develop is that of getting the other person's view of a situation before you express your own. However, if you only go through the motions and don't really listen to what is said – verbally and nonverbally – you are wasting a valuable tool. Seeing the situation from someone else's perspective means sincerely trying to crawl inside that person's head and to understand where he's coming from. It requires an attitude of sincere interest and concern, which is not something you can fake. You either care or you don't.

Demonstrate respect

You may see your boss, subordinate, or peer as a "difficult person", but it is a far better idea to view him or her as a unique individual who deserves your respect. Too often, in the day-to-day stresses of the work world, we lose sight of people's individuality. In the long run, even if you fail to come to an agreement, that does not make that person any less of a human being, and, as such, he or she is entitled to respect.

SIX STEPS TO DEMONSTRATING RESPECT

- Show a willingness to take part in the conversation.
- Pay attention, make eye contact, and listen carefully.
- Do not interrupt, disparage, or negate what is said.
- Clarify or summarize, as objectively as possible, what you think you heard.
- Find an area of agreement before you state your own view.
- Keep an open mind; be willing to change your position.

Plan and set the scene

A meeting is the tip of the iceberg. What really counts is the part you can't see – what is beneath the surface. What is invisible to the eye but critical to smooth sailing is planning. More meetings go astray or worse due to lack of thoughtful planning than because of unexpected events in the meeting itself.

If you have decided that a meeting is a sound strategy, how you make it happen will depend on the status of the other person. If you are the boss, you can call the meeting and assume the person will attend. If the other participant is a peer, you can only suggest and use persuasive benefit statements. And finally, if you want to meet with your boss, request the meeting in an assertive, non-adversarial tone.

Prepare yourself

Once you have agreed to a meeting, don't wing it. Plan, in advance, how you will approach each step, what you will want to say, how you will handle emotion and other negative responses, and what outcomes you hope to achieve. Write it down. Rehearse, if necessary. After all, this is a meeting with high stakes. A professional always prepares for a presentation; and, in terms of expressing your personal perspective on the matter, that's just what this is – a presentation.

Set the scene

Reduce stress. If you begin the discussion by clarifying your purpose, you not only minimize that stress, you focus the conversation immediately. On the other hand, if the other person has requested this meeting, your opening statement will ensure that you are addressing the correct topic.

If you initiate the meeting, your opening statement should begin with the word I: "I would like to discuss… I have some ideas on… I'm concerned about…"

If you are responding to a request for this meeting, your opening statement should begin with something like: "As I understand what you want to discuss today, it is…"

CHECKLIST FOR PLANNING A DIFFICULT MEETING

☐ **Clearly define your objective**

☐ **Request the meeting in a manner that is appropriate to the person and the problem**

☐ **Review the ten-step format and customize each of those steps to this specific person and situation**

☐ **Write out the questions you will ask and the points you wish to make**

☐ **Plan what you will do in the event of a positive or negative outcome**

Check willingness to talk

You have stated the problem as you see it or responded to the problem someone else has brought to your attention. That was your opening. At this point you are most probably convinced that this conversation should be held and that now is the time to hold it. You have done all your homework, centred yourself, and are now ready to talk things through. But what happens if the other half of this duo is not so ready? How can you tell if he or she isn't ready to talk?

Is the other person ready?

Often you will know at first glance whether your discussion partner is willing to talk. If the other person's body language is screaming at you – arms folded, facial expression hostile and body stiff – they aren't ready to talk. If you're not sure, ask.

After you state your understanding of the problem, using "I" sentences, you might say: "If this is a good time for you, I'd like to take a few minutes to talk about it. How do you feel about doing that now?"

If the response is direct – "Sure, that's fine with me," or "This isn't a good time. I'm in the middle of something," the answer is clear. But if the words say, "Sure, that's fine with me," and the body language and nonverbal cues say, "Don't kid yourself into thinking you're going to convince me of anything!" you have the proverbial mixed message. When in doubt, believe the nonverbal message rather than the verbal one. It's much easier to lie with words than with gestures, especially since few of us realize how much we are communicating through facial expressions, posture, and movements.

If this is not the right time

What can you do if you realize that one of you is not ready to talk? If you're upset or your discussion partner is unwilling, postpone the discussion. You won't accomplish a thing by going ahead with it.

"Give prior warning of meetings"

Confirm your understanding

Before you begin trying to resolve your difficulties with the other person, make sure that you have met to talk about the same issue. Do you both know why you are there? Check that you have a common purpose. Spell out the problem as you see it. Be specific. Focus on behaviour or results, not personality or opinion.

Get agreement on the problem

While it may seem apparent to you that you have adequately and accurately described the problem from your point of view, you may be surprised to discover that the other person doesn't see the problem in the same way at all.

Before you even begin, you have reached the first impasse. You need to reach an agreement on the nature of the problem before you can move on to trying to resolve it. For example, you may have a difficult working relationship with someone because they continually interrupt you when you are running meetings, making you

HERE ARE SOME EXAMPLES OF SETTING OUT EXACTLY WHAT THE PROBLEM IS

- As I recall, we agreed that you would limit your lunch breaks to exactly 45 minutes, so that I could leave on time for my lunch break. Every day this week, I have had 10-15 minutes cut off of my break, because you returned late, and I had to be back on time so that Charles could take his break.
- When we last talked, you said you would meet your sales-call quota for the month of March and thereafter for the rest of the year. It is now June, and you have fallen short of the required number of sales call every month since we spoke.

look incompetent in front of colleagues. However, the other person may think that the problem is they do not have enough opportunity to get their issues onto meeting agendas or that you do not call upon them in meetings. Because they don't get to speak, their point of view is not heard. After each stating your understanding of the problem, if you can agree that there is a general problem which results in each of you not being heard in meetings, you can then move on and try to resolve the issues raised. Bear in mind that if you and your peer or boss or employee readily agreed on things, you probably wouldn't be having this discussion in the first place. You don't see eye to eye on almost any subject, so it should be no surprise that you can't agree on the nature of the problem. Before you can go on you must come to a mutual understanding of what you are trying to resolve.

Stating your case

If you have called the meeting, your first step will be to state its purpose as you understand it, and to secure agreement from the other person on that purpose. Take a straightforward approach by saying, "The reason I wanted to get together is to discuss the

DESCRIBE THE SITUATION

Once you have agreed on the issue at hand, your purpose is to help the other person understand exactly what you're talking about and to accept it as meaningful. When describing behaviour or circumstances stick to the following guidelines.

- Be specific.
- Focus on things you have witnessed, rather than on your opinion or second-hand information.
- Refer to a particular action or event.
- Review when and where it took place, who was involved, and what results you personally observed.
- If the feedback is negative, do not deliver a litany of criticisms.
- Deal with one issue at a time.
- Don't dump your feelings of frustration on your boss, subordinate or co-worker.

importance of sticking to our agreed 45-minutes for lunch breaks. As I see it, when one of us leaves or returns late, it throws everyone's schedule off. Do you agree that this is a problem and that we are here to try to find a solution?" If you don't get agreement, continuing will be fruitless. Instead, back up until you both agree on the issue and the need to resolve it now.

Let the other person talk

Get the other person's perspective on the problem. When you get to this point, stop the action for a moment. Don't take for granted that the other person understands or accepts what you have just said. It's probably safe to assume that they do not. Your aim is to be sure that they recognize that there is a problem and agree to discuss it. Clarify why this issue is important enough to call this meeting and why you think your expectations are reasonable and fair.

Listen for understanding

This is something that most people rarely do. We are so intent on telling our side of the story that we blurt it out immediately, often catching the other person unawares and making them feel attacked without provocation.

This is the most important step in the process. The other person has feelings and a point of view. Find out what they are. Ask and listen – really listen. Don't interrupt, respond, explain, clarify, or defend your position. See if there is a problem in your department or your operating style. Try to understand his or her point.

Give the other person a chance to respond without threat of repercussions. Create a safe environment to do so.

Ask questions such as:

- How do you see this situation?
- What are your feelings or reactions to what I've just said?
- I'd really like to hear your views on this. Tell me what you think.

Ask questions to clarify the other person's point of view

Don't assume that, because you've asked a couple of questions, you truly know or comprehend the other side of the story. If you got any information at all, at one extreme it was probably superficial and at the other exaggerated. In either case, if you really want to understand where your discussion partner is coming from, you'll have to keep digging. Here is where questions, summary statements and reflections come into the picture.

One way to find out more is to ask simple, straightforward questions, of which there are two kinds. Open questions encourage a full and uninhibited response.

- What was your view of this situation?
- How do you think we could solve the problem?

Closed questions limit the answers to one of two words, yes or no, or agreement or disagreement.

- Was Jane there at the time?

- Did you follow up on that assignment?
- Do you think the project was a failure?

Feed back both content and emotions

One of the most effective ways of getting to the heart of any matter is to give feedback on what you heard, saw, or sensed. In one case, you summarize content; in the other, you reflect back the other person's emotions.

Summary statements are not meant to parrot what you heard in the person's exact words. Rather, they are meant to check the accuracy and meaning of what you heard, in your own words.

Reflecting back emotions gets behind the words to unspoken feelings and intentions. Reflection requires all of your senses – listening for tone, inflection, volume, sincerity; watching the body language and spotting the nonverbal cues; and intuitively getting a sense of the truth. In this case, it's not what is said but how it is said and in what context.

Get the whole message

Use summary statements. When you summarize or paraphrase, you are verifying the content and meaning of what you heard, as you understand them. If you are wrong, you'll find out instantly and can then revise your understanding; if you are right, you will probably gain additional information. In either case, you will know if you are on the right track. If you didn't get the other person's message, start over until you do.

- Let me be sure I got this right. You delegated the project to Tom, who agreed to have it done by Monday afternoon, but missed the deadline. Correct?
- As I understand what you just said, you informed me of today's meeting last week and assumed I had put it on my calendar, and when I didn't attend you were very disappointed. Is that the gist of it?

Use reflecting statements

When you reflect or mirror back what you heard, observed or sensed, you are exploring feelings and emotions, as you interpret them. This is more complex than summarizing because people don't always know what nonverbal messages they are sending. It may be obvious to you that someone is angry or nervous, but they may not be aware of this. You could say:

- This seems to be a difficult subject for you to discuss.
- You seem really uncomfortable.

Look for areas of agreement

Think of areas of agreement as the bridge over troubled waters. If you can truly hear what the other person has to say and find something with which you can agree, you will meet each other in the middle of that bridge.

After you have heard the other person out and feel that you have their side of the story – their impressions, reactions, or opinions – you're probably more than ready to have your say. But don't do it; there is one more step to take.

It takes patience and perseverance to remain quiet and let someone else talk, but it is the key to success in a potentially confrontational encounter. Actually, it the key to success in any encounter.

The next step may not be easy either, but it is equally important. If you have really been listening with an open mind, you have surely heard at least one thing upon which the two of you can agree. You may even have uncovered more than one. This is the bridge-building step – your chance to point out these overlapping areas and to try to establish some common ground on which you can resolve more difficult issues.

This step accomplishes two things: it demonstrates that you were open to the other person's point of view and that there are indeed areas of agreement to build on.

EXAMPLES

- I absolutely agree with you that some of our procedures are time-consuming and bureaucratic and that we would be much more efficient if we could eliminate some of this red tape.
- I do see your point on the brainstorming process at yesterday's meeting. You're correct in observing that what we did was not brainstorming; it was more of a free-for-all.
- I hadn't looked at it that way before, but your perspective on the plan really is interesting. Tell me a little more about it.
- While I do have some strong opinions on how this should be done, it seems that you do as well. I'd like to know your rationale for doing it that way. Maybe I haven't looked at this from every angle.

State your position

Now it's your turn. You have stated the problem, checked for willingness to go on, verified that you are both dealing with the same problem, heard the other person out, and built a bridge from their side to yours. Now it is time for you walk across the bridge, so to speak.

Present "your side of the story" as clearly and unemotionally as possible. Then offer some ideas of how the situation might be remedied (if you are dealing with one that requires remedying).

Whenever possible, use concrete examples or ideas. Don't speak in vague generalities. If you have found that certain approaches to this problem have worked for you in the past, it may be useful to offer them as possible approaches to the current situation.

It is also possible that having heard the other perspective there may have been a change in yours, which will alter the way you present it.

Most important, don't berate, accuse or blame, and try not to start sentences with "you"; start them with "I".

■ **Be specific**
■ **Don't blame**
■ **Don't shout**

EXAMPLES

■ Don, while I do agree with you on the three points I just mentioned, there are some areas I see quite differently. One is that, even though our procedures are very flawed, we can't just throw them out the window and decide on a case-by-case basis how to handle every situation or crisis. In my view, we need guidelines of some kind. If our current ones are inadequate, what would you think of rewriting them? Perhaps we could do that together.

■ Your approach to the plan does make a lot of sense, and I can see why you're so keen on it. But I think you've overlooked something. I'd like to tell you what I think it is.

■ I'll admit that is an angle I never even considered; and, while it does sound convincing, I'd like to share with you some of the benefits of my approach.

Talk through problem areas

Talking through your differences is clearly the toughest step – one that will require all the communication skills at your disposal. Don't hesitate to use them!

It's unrealistic to think that, just because you've got this far, you're home free. There are bound to be topics on which you are still miles apart, or at least appear to be.

This is the heart of the discussion. Your purpose after all is to reach an agreement – a win:win agreement. If you don't get through this step with honesty and open-mindeness, you will not achieve your purpose.

SOME GUIDELINES FOR RESOLVING DIFFERENCES

■ Review the section in Chapter 2 on practicing assertive communication. Remember to show respect for yourself and for the other person. Don't take an aggressive stance, and don't cave in.

■ State the other person's opposing position and have her state yours. It's amazing how quickly you come to understand where someone is coming from when you articulate her point of view. Sometimes, this is all that is necessary.

■ Stress benefits. Ask yourself what she will gain if she changes her stance, and point out that benefit to her. Every good salesperson uses benefits to sell an idea, a service, or a product.

■ Stay focused on win:win. If you can't get that far, settle for compromise; but under no circumstances settle for win:lose or lose:lose. If you find yourself at an dead end, call time out, regroup, and try it again later.

Consider extenuating circumstances

Don't rush to judgment or capitulate without exploring the possibility of extenuating circumstance, such as work load, relationships and conflicts with co-workers, or personal problems at home. Talk about them. Dig a little. The strain between you may be little more than a symptom of something else. If that "something else" can be remedied, you may have a win:win situation.

Be prepared to refer elsewhere

By considering extenuating circumstances, you may uncover a problem of which you were unaware and that is beyond your ability to solve. It may be that your subordinate or peer has a personal problem that is so troubling it is causing his performance to suffer. If you know of a resource that might be helpful, suggest it.

If he is a co-worker, and all suggestions have been rebuffed, but there is a personal problem that will continue to affect his performance at work, you may have to talk to your manager or go to Human Resources for help and advice.

If you are open, the other person may share their problem; but do not play the role of amateur psychologist. All you want is enough information to make a wise referral.

Resolve the issue

Develop an action plan between you. The goal of this discussion is to look for a way to improve whatever is going badly. By this time, you and the other person have exchanged points of view, candidly discussed those areas where you were not in agreement, and sincerely sought a mutually beneficial solution.

If you agree that there is a problem and what it is, the next step is to ask, "What can we do to solve it?"

This should be done collaboratively. If you impose your plan on a recalcitrant employee or peer, it will merely serve as a stop-gap measure. Eventually, you'll both be back where you began – uncooperative at least, downright hostile at most.

The action plan should spell out what is to be done, by whom, under what conditions and by what date. If you develop this plan together, you are far more likely to get agreement and participation, which is precisely what you want. If you impose the plan, it is likely to backfire or simply not be carried out.

Check the other person's perception of the agreement

It's important at this point to be sure you are both on the same frequency. Ask the other person to verbalize their understanding of what you have agreed to. Put it in writing if you like and both of you sign it. Just be sure that you both walk away with the same understanding of your plan.

Summarize the meeting

Two people rarely see things from the same perspective. While you may assess the meeting and its conclusions one way, it's very possible the other person sees it entirely differently. One of your last steps should be to ask the other person to summarize her view of what happened and what was agreed. If your views are different, this is the time to find out and set the record straight.

Express your support

Once you have agreed on the content and results of your discussion, end the meeting on a positive note. Let the other person know that you too are committed to a successful outcome and that you are confident he has the ability to carry out the plan. Offer your assistance if it's needed. Tie up the session in an upbeat, supportive manner. The other person's last impression of your support will make a lasting impression that could well tip the scales in favour of a positive resolution. You may even end up becoming allies.

Follow through

All the planning and execution in the world is wasted if there is no follow through.

When the deadline you both agreed upon comes around sit down and carefully analyze the results. Ask the following:

- Did the action plan work?
- If not, why not?
- Has the other person had every opportunity to make the necessary changes, and has she made them?

If the situation you are dealing with is part of a formal disciplinary procedure and the person involved has not met the criteria set in the action plan, this may mean that you decide to fire them.

If this person is a peer, you don't have the authority to get rid of them; but you do have the option of bringing this matter to the attention of your manager, or the Human Resources Department. When you have done all that you can do, seek help through the proper channels, particularly if the problem could have legal ramifications.

A good rule of thumb is, when in doubt, don't take chances. In today's litigious environment, it is better to be safe than sorry. Seek expert advice or better still, ask the most appropriate person or department to handle it on your behalf.

FIRING SOMEONE

- Do it cleanly
- Do it quickly
- Pick your time
- Do not fire someone on a Friday afternoon
- Explain the reasons
- Be specific – "We agreed on this course of action and you have not lived up to it".
- If you are in a position to offer assistance, such as outplacement counselling, use of the office and equipment or the phone – spell those things out and build them into the termination process.

Try something different

Of course, not every situation is an all-or-nothing scenario that must end in compliance or dismissal. These are extremes that are not always appropriate. If you are the person's supervisor you have other tools at your disposal besides exercising your authority or terminating the person. One manager recalls a situation in which nothing seemed to work, including warnings of dismissal. This manager sensed that his subordinate was neither stupid nor hopeless. He was sure that there had to be some way to break through to this employee, and he was determined to find it. Here is how he recalls the process:

"Mary Anne was 'difficult' in that she didn't communicate. I never knew if she couldn't or just wouldn't, but getting a whole sentence out of her was like pulling teeth. She would sulk and avoid the subject, or she would agree to anything I suggested and then do none of it. Her attitude seemed to be, 'This isn't my problem, this isn't part of my job, this isn't the way we've done it in the past.' Her unspoken message was, 'Don't rock the boat.'

It would have been so easy to blow up or give up, and I came close a couple of times until I analysed her behaviour

a little more. My strategy for enlisting her cooperation had several steps:

- Keeping the changes I wanted her to make simple and brief; breaking them down into increments; and presenting them to her one at a time instead of in a batch.
- Removing the sense of urgency and making sure my voice was unthreatening, my pace was slow, and my demeanor as low key as I could manage.
- Taking the time to work with her to get each step in writing so that I knew we both had the same understanding of the task.
- Checking with her on an informal basis from time to time (not too frequently or regularly) to see how she was doing.
- Complimenting her on her successes, not berating her for lapses, and keeping my delivery as unemotional as possible.
- Offering encouragement with benefits that were relevant to her needs, which were to keep things stable and familiar, stay within her job responsibilities, and keep her out of the spotlight.

The strategy worked, but slowly, and it required a great deal of discipline and patience, which were not my strongest suits at the time."

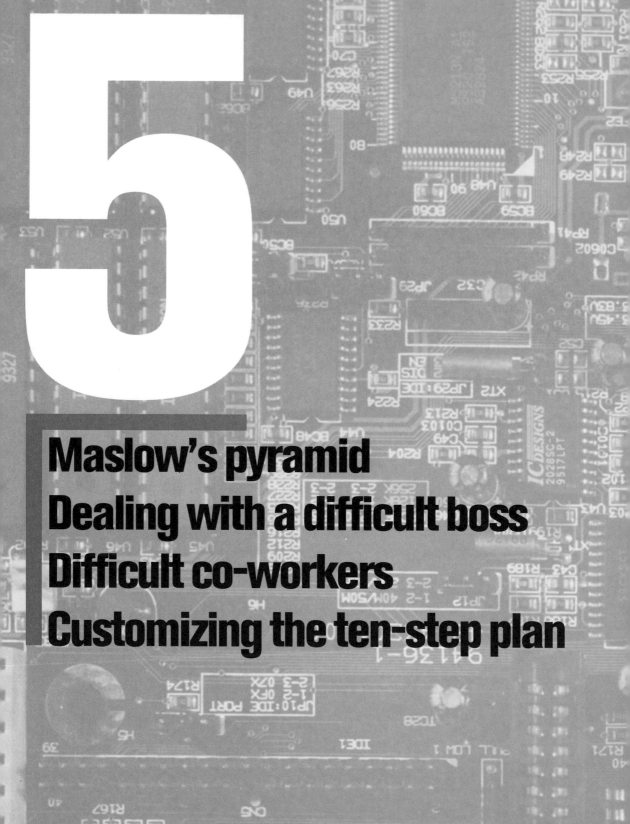

5

Maslow's pyramid
Dealing with a difficult boss
Difficult co-workers
Customizing the ten-step plan

How can a behaviour model help?
What are the other person's needs?
How can I adapt to the situation?

Maslow's pyramid

Virtually every book on dealing with people – no matter who they are, no matter what your relationship with them and no matter what the circumstances – makes some reference to "Maslow's pyramid of needs". The renowned psychologist Abraham Maslow identified seven basic human needs and stacked them from the most basic to the most esoteric.

Human beings are motivated to act based on their most urgent, unfulfilled needs at the moment. There are a number of interpretations regarding the order of this pyramid. That shown below is the best known.

If we are unhappy with how things are going on level one, we are unlikely to care very much about moving up the pyramid to level two. In other words, if

Abraham Maslow, Hierarchy of needs (1964)

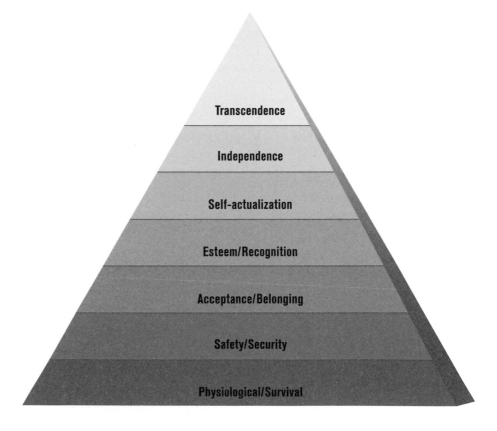

Transcendence

Independence

Self-actualization

Esteem/Recognition

Acceptance/Belonging

Safety/Security

Physiological/Survival

our most basic physical needs for food and shelter are not met, we can think of little else. When we are well fed and housed, we can then begin to focus on safety needs.

Physiological/Survival

These needs are fundamental and biological in nature. They include the minimum conditions that our bodies must have in order to survive and function properly. They include the basic requirements of food, drink, shelter, sex, sleep, or recovery from injury or illness.

To fulfill these most fundamental needs at work, people must have adequate pay; opportunities to take breaks; and a safe, healthy work environment.

Safety/Security

We all need to know with some certainty that the world in which we live is enduring and predictable and that we are safe from harm.

Security needs include protection from violence or chaos, a sense of order and stability, and the absence of fear.

To feel secure at work, employees need to see that safety is a management priority, that there is predictability to rules and regulations, that the company is stable and that the atmosphere is one of civility and reason.

Acceptance/Belonging

Our social needs encompass companionship, love, affection, and inclusion in a group. These needs are satisfied through support from others, harmonious relationships, friendship, and being part of a community.

At work, such needs are met by a spirit of collaboration and teamwork in which people are encouraged to work together, as opposed to competing.

Esteem/Recognition

Reputation, status, and prestige fulfil our esteem needs, as do approval, self-respect, and a feeling of worth. Satisfaction of these needs is expressed by respect from others in our personal and professional lives; a sense of mastery; and acknowledgment, praise or reward for our achievements.

Independence

Independence needs focus on privacy, individuality, responsibility and self-determination. We want the chance to run our own lives; to feel in control; to be proactive, as opposed to reactive; and to rely on our own ability to get things done. Autonomy means being empowered to do one's job without undue pressure or control; self-determination implies being in charge of one's own career and success.

Maslow's pyramid

Self-actualization

Also called self-realization and self-fulfilment, these needs refer to becoming all that we are capable of being – reaching our fullest potential. They represent the human drive to develop and use our personal resources to grow, learn and mature; and to increase our sense of control over life.

People with self-actualization needs must be challenged and must excel. They are not satisfied with merely putting in their hours or getting the job done, and must be encouraged to exceed expectations.

Transcendence

This is our spiritual dimension. It surpasses reaching our own potential to encompass the pursuit of beauty, wisdom, a deeper understanding of the world, and a sense of connection with the divine. It is possible to have transcendence needs met in a work environment. Anything that permits people to reach out to each other, to continue to seek and to learn is a step in the direction of filling this need.

Why match attitudes and behaviour to need?

If you understand the needs of other people, you will know what "makes people tick" and why they act as they do. If you know where they are on the pyramid, you will have more idea about what it takes to reach and to motivate them. This in turn may give you more opportunity to create a more harmonious working relationship with them. These needs can be applied to any of the other behaviour models.

Case study

As an example, consider a person who fits the "REACTIVE (INDECISIVE) + PEOPLE-ORIENTED" profile opposite. What value would it have to infer that person's needs from his behaviour? You know many of the things in the behaviour box apply: that he doesn't like to make decisions, get people mad at him or bask in the spotlight. You know that he has a need for acceptance, to belong and to be liked. If you wanted to influence that person, to smooth out a difficult relationship or to get his cooperation, you would let him know how much the team depends on his participation. While you do nothing to offend or hurt him, at the same time you might suggest that people in the department, including you, like teammates who get along and go along – one of the traits he has always exhibited. You use questions to get to his real feelings and to arrive at agreement on the issue.

Getting the whole picture

In the boxes below are the basic behaviour prototypes, based on four tendencies: proactivity (top two boxes); reactivity (bottom two boxes); lack of concern for people (left-hand boxes); and concern for people (right-hand boxes). Use these tools to understand what "makes people tick."

If we add needs and behaviours to these attitudes, we create the whole picture.

PROACTIVE (CONTROLLING) + NO CONCERN FOR PEOPLE

BEHAVIOURS: Take charge, run the show, be a star, grab the credit... do what it takes to get your way, likely to lose your temper when you don't... use anger as a club

NEEDS: Esteem/recognition, independence

PROACTIVE (DECISIVE) + PEOPLE ORIENTED

BEHAVIOURS: Lead, take on tough decisions and challenges... share the spotlight, control the situation, not the people... listen to input... do what you feel is best... stay in control... stay focused on the task

NEEDS: Independence, self-actualization

REACTIVE (PASSIVE) + NO CONCERN FOR PEOPLE

BEHAVIOURS: Shun responsibility, confrontation and the spotlight... keep your thoughts and feelings to yourself... accept bad treatment but then fume inwardly, sulk or pout... don't volunteer ideas or opinions

NEEDS: Safety/security

REACTIVE (INDECISIVE) + PEOPLE ORIENTED

BEHAVIOURS: Don't like to make decisions, get people angry, be a leader or a star... like to be a team player, let others shine... tell people more than they want or need to know... get hurt easily

NEEDS: Acceptance/belonging

Difficult bosses

We all tend to put bosses in two categories, effective and difficult. Effective bosses enhance your ability to do your job, recognize your achievements and focus on what is best for the department or work group. Difficult bosses promote discord, undermine effort and diminish those who report to them.

The impact your boss has on your life is inestimable. Of all the potentially stressful workplace relationships, few can be as agonizing as one with a difficult boss.

While many people believe that most bosses aren't terribly effective, the really bad ones may actually inflict damage on their employees. Difficult bosses are so pervasive that they have widely accepted labels by which their behaviour instantly can be recognized.

There are all kinds of ways of looking at your relationship with your boss. You can see this person as someone who has complete power over your work life. Another is to see him or her as an annoyance to be endured. Alternatively, assume this is a partner, with whom you work to bring benefit to both of you and the company.

How you view your boss depends on many factors: his or her style, your style, the culture in which you work, your previous experiences with other bosses and the nature of your work.

Bosses may have held management positions in the past, but chances are they have developed their management style by the seat of their pants over the years. Management training is a plus but not necessarily a guarantee of competence.

A DIFFICULT BOSS MAY:
- hog the credit and the spotlight
- intimidate employees
- patronize employees
- make people so miserable that they quit
- sabotage careers
- talk about people behind their backs
- play one-upmanship
- be threatened by smart or talented subordinates
- give no feedback
- gloss over problems
- magnify problems
- pass on top management's dictums
- refuse to talk
- refuse to play

AN EFFECTIVE BOSS WILL:
- have basic people skills and use them
- communicate clearly and directly
- help you set and attain goals
- take the time to listen to you
- delegate work and then get out of your way and let you do it
- respect herself and you
- be a risk-taker
- build esprit de corps and encourage teamwork
- bring a sense of purpose to the department or work group

THE DICTATOR

Some dictators are the way they are because this is the only management style they have ever been exposed to, and because top management condones this style because it gets results. Others are simply angry people who have never learned to control their emotions or to channel their anger constructively.

ATTITUDES
proactive (controlling) + no concern for people

BEHAVIOURS
- take charge
- run the show
- be a star
- grab the credit
- take all the bows
- do what it takes to get their way
- likely to lose temper when don't get their own way
- use anger as a club

NEEDS
- esteem/recognition
- independence

HOW TO DEAL WITH A DICTATOR
- Try to prove your value to someone else in the organization who may appreciate your abilities and go to bat for you.
- Talk it out with a person you can trust.
- Seek help from the Human Resources Department.
- If this is a harassment issue, seek legal advice.

Difficult bosses

If your boss can't manage her way out of paper bag, you are probably frustrated much of the time. Besides wondering how in the world she got this far in the company, you may be quite sure you could do her job better than she's doing it. Her problem is fear; a bumbler always feels at risk.

THE BUMBLER

As this boss muddles through the day, avoiding decisions, barely communicating and doing her best not to make waves, your department drifts along like a rudderless boat. She is trying not to be noticed, to just blend in with the furniture. She is afraid a more capable person on her staff might displace her, afraid that if she makes a decision it will be the wrong one, afraid she will blamed for any mistake one of her people makes.

ATTITUDES
reactive (passive) + no concern for people

BEHAVIOURS
- shuns responsibility, confrontation and the spotlight
- keeps thoughts and feelings to his/herself
- accepts bad treatment but then fumes inwardly, sulks or pouts
- doesn't offer ideas or opinions

NEEDS
- safety/security

HOW TO DEAL WITH A BUMBLER
- Try to determine what others see in this person without contributing to the rumour mill.
- Try to get a feel of the security of this person's position in the organization.
- Don't be the cause of embarrassment.
- Keep this boss shielded from situations that might reveal weaknesses.
- Take on more responsibility
- Document your work as evidence of your capabilities.
- Apply for another job within the company.
- Talk to someone you trust in the Human Resources Department.
- Consider going elsewhere.

THE PARENT

This is the boss who feels a great sense of responsibility for his little group of employees, just as he does for his children; and he runs the same tight ship at the office as the one at home. On one hand he is a tough taskmaster – exacting, demanding, often disapproving. On the other hand, he becomes totally sympathetic when you are sick – insisting that you go home, recommending doctors and doing everything but bringing you chicken soup. The problem is, you are not his child; you are his subordinate. If he views you as one of his kids, he is not treating you as an equal or as a competent adult.

ATTITUDES
reactive (indecisive) + people oriented

BEHAVIOURS
- doesn't like to make decisions, get people angry, be a leader or a star
- does like to be a team player
- lets others shine
- tells people more than they want or need to know
- gets hurt easily

NEEDS
- acceptance/belonging

HOW TO DEAL WITH A "PARENT"
- Never slip into childish behaviour.
- Keep your emotions under control.
- Keep your cool even in the middle of a confrontation.
- Be appropriately respectful but not obsequious.
- Maintain your sense of self.
- Don't let the conversation get too personal; keep it on a professional level.

Difficult bosses

The cheerleader is one of those rare people who simply attract us, draw us in and turn us on. Such people have a special presence about them, a kind of magnetism. Their energy is quite literally contagious and their effect inspiring. If they use this gift for the benefit of their people and the company, they are worth their weight in gold.

THE CHEERLEADER

A cheerleader can iron out any disagreement, forge you and your co-workers into a cohesive team, see your potential even when you don't see it, and help your career in many ways. She can be a wonderful mentor, praise you for a job well done, help you overcome weaknesses, and shine the spotlight on you. But although she is a born leader, she isn't always a team player and while she can see the big picture, she may become bored by the details.

ATTITUDES
proactive (decisive) + people oriented

BEHAVIOURS
- leads the charge, makes tough decisions, takes on challenges, shares the spotlight, controls the situation but not people
- listens and considers input
- does what she feels is best
- doesn't run roughshod over people
- doesn't lose control
- stays focused

NEEDS
- independence/ self-actualization

HOW TO DEAL WITH A CHEERLEADER
- Be honest and up front.
- Provide feedback on how you feel, how others feel and what's going on in your department.
- Share your knowledge, talent, information and expertise.
- Be proactive, self-empowered and self-motivated.
- Become an expert at details.
- Always make this boss look good.
- Consistently provide support and reinforcement within the organization.
- Be a fan. Be a cheerleader.

A SPECIAL CASE: THE ADDICTED BOSS

How do you know if your boss is abusing drugs or alcohol? Here are some clues:

- inexplicable behaviour, particularly after lunch
- lateness in the morning or prone to miss Mondays
- lack of the old sharpness
- napping on the job
- inappropriate sharing of personal or financial difficulties
- erratic and frequent mood swings
- uncharacteristic verbal abuse
- obvious and unusual depression
- the smell of alcohol
- excessive drinking at company events

HOW TO DEAL WITH AN ADDICT

- Realize the volatility of this situation and your position in it.
  Be careful; don't put either of you at risk.
- Don't diagnose the problem.
- Maintain an attitude of concern and compassion for your boss.
- If your company has an Employee Assistance Programme, request an appointment; lay out your concerns, supported by documented facts, and ask for help.
- Seek help from someone you trust in the Human Resources Department
  As a last resort request a private meeting with your boss, talk about your observations, keep the conversation focused on facts and behaviours and express your concerns. (This is difficult and risky.)

Difficult peers

In your relationship with peers neither of you has any real "power" over the other. In theory, you enjoy equal status. But when this person marches to a different drummer, has a wide streak of independence, prefers competition to collaboration, or is just plain antisocial, you have a problem.

Even if you were not trying to create a collaborative work environment, your problem could be just trying to coexist on the same planet with a very difficult person – someone with whom you can find no common ground and who seems bent on making your life at work a living hell.

Take heart. There are ways to work with this person and, though you may never be best friends, at least you can avoid being worst enemies. The downside of course is that you have no clout; on the other hand, neither does she. So, you start level.

Don't psychoanalyze

You are not a therapist; and it is inappropriate to act like one. If you had 100 guesses, you would probably not guess what is really going on in your co-worker's mind.

If you are willing to give him or her the benefit of the doubt, you could assume one of two things: either something is going on outside of work and their behaviour has nothing to do with you; or your relationship has deteriorated, and their behaviour has everything to do with you.

Confront the issue

The only way to know what is wrong is to ask, which is probably the last thing you want to do. But if you are able to, try to say something that is not an attack on him or his behaviour, such as, "I sense some tension between us, which I would very much like to resolve. If I have done anything to offend you, please tell me what it is, so that we can clear the air between us."

The best possible outcome may be that he may tell you that you have done nothing and that he has things on his mind, or that you have done something and what it is. The worst possible outcome would be that you get no new information; but at least you gave it your best shot.

SUMMARY

- Don't psychoanalyze.
- Confront the issue.
- Don't get personal.
- Stick to the issues.
- Remember to be assertive.
- Build a support system.

Don't get personal

The best way to exacerbate a problem is to personalize it. Either you take the conversation personally and get your feelings hurt or you attack the other person and hurt their feelings.

Statements such as, "You have an attitude problem," or "You are an information bottleneck who is slowing down the entire department," or, "We lost the account because you missed the deadline," are blaming, attacking statements. The word "you" should alert you to restrain; rethink; and, if possible, reword.

Stick to the issues

Sometimes it is hard to separate the issue from the person involved in the issue, but it's important to try. Focus on the problem, the policy, the area of disagreement; do not focus on personal traits. It's fine to voice strong emotions, but they have to be carefully packaged. It isn't dishonest to package your remarks; it is diplomatic and smart. People can accept tough talk if it's delivered the right way.

Be assertive

When we are angry or frustrated it is easy to forget everything we ever knew about assertive communication. Our tendency is to become aggressive and dominate the other person or to become passive and capitulate without a fight. In the middle is keeping our heads and being assertive, neither of which come naturally in the heat of battle. Remember that assertiveness is built on a foundation of respect: respect for yourself and respect for the other person. If you cultivate those two attitudes you will always communicate in the right way. If you respect yourself, you won't become defensive and cave in. In fact, you won't allow yourself to be attacked. If you respect the other person, you won't go on the offensive. Rather, you will find some way to state your position without belittling the other person in the process.

Build a support system

There are times when you will need others to help you through a tough situation. Calling on team members for short-term support is quite different from putting together a permanent group of allies to back you up in your ongoing battle with another person. First of all, you shouldn't be engaged in an ongoing battle. Office feuds are costly in terms of energy, morale, and productivity. It takes two to feud. You have no control over your co-worker, but you do have control of yourself. You can refuse to play the game.

Difficult employees

ifficult employees are here to stay and present some unique challenges. Returning to the model of attitudes, behaviours, and needs, it is easy to see how the same factors can help you understand those who report to you. Consider these descriptions in terms of your employees. Once again, if you know what they need, you know how to manage them.

THE STAR

The star might as well be saying, "pay attention to me, listen to me, shower me with accolades, and give me room to do my own thing."

ATTITUDES

proactive (controlling) + no concern for people

BEHAVIOURS

- wants to win; poor loser
- takes all the credit; aims for centre stage; doesn't share the spotlight
- turns the slightest remark into an insult
- interrupts, dominates conversations
- makes sweeping statements; takes a strong stand on every issue
- values position and status symbols
- does poorly in team situations
- boasts and brags about accomplishments

NEEDS

- esteem/recognition/independence

HOW TO DEAL WITH A STAR

- Let her take the credit for positive results; praise her in public.
- Let her vent, especially when she is hot under the collar.
- Ignore aggressively challenging questions or statements.
- Ask for advice or suggestions.
- Give her tangible evidence of appreciation such as a better office or a raise.

THE MOLE

The Mole seems to be saying, "Don't pay attention to me, don't ask me anything, keep me out of the limelight, just tell me what to do."

"Draw the person out by asking questions"

ATTITUDES

reactive (passive) + no concern for people

BEHAVIOURS

- shuns responsibility, confrontation and the spotlight
- keeps thoughts and feelings to him/herself
- accepts bad treatment but fumes inwardly, sulks or pouts
- doesn't offer ideas or opinions
- plays his cards close to his chest
- stays neutral in disputes
- lacks self-confidence, apologizes a lot
- wants to work alone; remote
- follows the rules; goes by the book
- adheres to tradition
- tends to be negative, pessimistic, overly cautious
- prefers to follow than to lead
- procrastinates

NEEDS

- safety/security

HOW TO DEAL WITH A MOLE

- Conduct discussions in private; keep them confidential; never embarrass him.
- Ask open questions for fuller responses.
- Put things in writing.
- Present ideas gradually, one at a time; avoid surprises.
- Make your directions absolutely clear; ask for a recap.
- Acknowledge that change is difficult.

Difficult employees

THE PARTNER
From the partner we might hear, "We should both be paying attention and listening to each other; give me responsibility and a challenge; lets get the job done."

ATTITUDES
proactive (decisive) + people oriented

BEHAVIOURS
- makes tough decisions; takes on challenges
- shares the spotlight
- controls the situation but not people
- listens and considers input
- does what they feel is best
- tackles tough issues and opposing views
- shares ideas, credit, the spotlight, responsibility
- cares about people and their needs
- seeks for information and understanding
- loves a challenge; easily bored
- focuses on the task at hand

NEEDS
- independence
- self-actualization

HOW TO DEAL WITH A PARTNER
- Carefully consider her ideas and suggestions.
- Earn their respect.
- Admit when you are wrong; apologize when you are.
- Offer an incentive for the most original, innovative solution to a problem.
- Go beyond delegation; empower them to take the ball and run with it.
- Be candid and straightforward; they can take it.
- Clarify the desired results; leave the method of achievement to them.

THE BUDDY

The Buddy is saying, "Please like me, listen to my stories, tell me how I can help you, let's have a good time and be friends."

ATTITUDES

reactive (indecisive) + people oriented

BEHAVIOURS

- doesn't like to make decisions, get people angry, be a leader or a star
  does like to be a team player
  lets others shine
- tells people more than they want or need to know
- gets hurt easily
- craves acceptance and to be liked
- can't stop talking
- likes people; is liked by people
  agrees, compromises, gives in easily
  has trouble making decisions

NEEDS

acceptance/belonging

HOW TO DEAL WITH A BUDDY

- Let him talk for a while.
- Keep the discussion on track when it wanders.
- Express interest; be sympathetic.
  Address him by name when you speak to him.
  Compliment liberally.
- Share a personal experience or confidence.
- Keep things light and upbeat.
- Let him know that other people like him
- Build extra time into your meetings.

In meetings

Meetings provide a critical link in the chain of communications in every organization. They are integral to the way business is conducted and information communicated. However, they can be a source of friction between people and raise problems, especially if people feel that their point of view is not being heard.

When you are leading the meeting

When you are conducting a meeting, how do you avoid runaway discussions in which the rules fly out the window, everyone talks at once, heated exchanges break out, and you lose control? If you don't prevent them and your carefully planned discussion runs amok, how can you rein it back in? When you see the discussion beginning to run away, try to step in, take control and stop it escalating. If you have to stop an argument that has already begun, you could interrupt and take the floor. You have several options.

- You could sum up what is going on. "This discussion seems to have taken on a life of its own. I can sum up each of your viewpoints. Then we can decide how to proceed."

TELEPHONE COMMUNICATION

You may have to deal with difficult people over the telephone. This deprives both parties of visual, nonverbal cues, such as body language and facial expression. To compensate, learn to listen attentively, to hear "between the lines".

- Prepare to listen. Clear your mind of other things and focus on listening.
- Turn away from your other work both physically and psychologically.
- Keep an open mind. Try to understand what the other person is saying.
- Let the other person say whatever they have to say without interruption. If they wander, bring them back on track with a question.
- Provide feedback to let the other person know that you hear them and that you understand.
- Sit as you would if that person were across your desk. Look in the mirror if necessary, and be sure your voice reflects a face that projects friendliness.
- Take notes during the call. Get the facts, but also record your impressions and reactions.
- Repeat and verify all key facts.

■ Alternatively, you could call on someone else to speak.
"Excuse me, but I'd like to hear from Adrienne on this. She headed up our last project and has a pretty good grasp of our style."

■ You could ask the combatants to sum up each other's point of view.
"So that we can clarify this issue, James, would you tell us what you think June is trying to say? If you're wrong, she can correct your misunderstanding. Then, we'll reverse the process and ask her what she thinks you are trying to say."

■ As a last resort, you could recess the meeting to give everyone a chance to cool down.
"Let's take a 15-minute break and give everyone a chance to sort out our feelings on this subject"

Keeping control

There are two kinds of control – self-control and meeting control. Self-control means that you keep your head, stay calm, and don't become part of the problem. Meeting control, on the other hand, focuses on controlling the meeting process, not the people at the meeting. Meeting control might involve the following:

■ intervening when the discussion drifts off course
■ clarifying fuzzy issues
■ summarizing the main points and finding a common thread among them
■ breaking up logjams or arguments
■ cutting off discussion on one topic to move on to another.

When you are attending the meeting

As a participant, you have less control than as a leader. If you are not happy with what is going on, silently think through and identify your feelings. What do you feel? Are your feelings valid? Should you express them? Examine your own behaviour and change it if necessary.

■ If you are talking too much, try giving others a chance to speak.
■ Pay attention, and speak up when you have something to say.
■ If you have assumed an adversarial role with another group member or with the chairperson, switch your tactics and assume a more supportive role.
■ Enlist the aid of fellow participants to bring about a change in the meeting; bring the difficult issue to the attention of the meeting leader; or throw it out on the table as a point for general discussion.

If you don't like the way a meeting is going, you have three options:
■ **You can leave.**
■ **You can accept it and adjust.**
■ **You can change it.**

Case study: customizing the steps

The ten-step process is the foundation. Now it is time to build a structure.

At this point, you have the necessary tools to work through a difficult situation with a particularly difficult person, the basic list of what to do and what not to do, a ten-step template for any discussion, and a way to appropriately customize those steps to an individual's needs and to your relationship with that person. Now, let's put those tools to work.

The scenario

If you had to assess your own style, you might use words like collaborative, team player, self-motivated, intellectually curious, and solution-oriented. You have an idea for a way to improve communications between your department (Marketing) and your sister department (Sales). Believing that they should be working hand in glove for the benefit of the company, you have developed a plan to bring this about. You need your manager's commitment to and support for your plan. Your past experience tells you that you'll get it, enthusiastically and immediately, but without much thought or substance. You want real commitment and help in selling your idea to senior management.

Observe the person's behaviour

Your boss is the quintessential mom. She loves everybody; everybody loves her; she treats her employees as if they were her kids. She's always bringing in home-baked cakes or taking everyone out to lunch. She'll listen to your problems for hours if that's what you need; she'll give you advice, send you home when you're sick, even watch your kids, if necessary. On the other hand, she will look so crestfallen when you fail to come through, you sometimes think she might just die of disappointment. Anything you do is great; any idea you have is terrific; any way she can help she will, except... she gets busy with someone else's problem or idea or request and forgets to follow through. This time you need her to remember and go to bat for your idea.

You also know she has a short attention span and can't seem to stay on one subject very long, especially if it is complex or detailed. She even jokes about it. This plan may take a while to explain thoroughly, and you can just imagine her eyes glazing over. You wonder how you will be able to keep her interested long enough to make your point.

Determine the person's needs

Here's what you know about her. She is definitely a parent-type boss.

■ Attitudes: Reactive (indecisive) + people oriented

■ Behaviours: Doesn't like to make decisions, get people angry, be a leader or a star... likes to be a team player... lets others shine... tells people more than necessary... easily hurt

■ Needs: Acceptance/belonging

On Maslow's pyramid of needs, she is on the "Acceptance/Belonging" level. Her behaviour tells you that she needs companionship, love, affection, support from others, harmonious relationships, friendship and inclusion in a group or on a team.

The danger here is typecasting her as if these were her only needs. While this is an effective device for understanding this person's principle motivators, it is a mistake to conclude that she has only one dimension.

Tailor your response to those needs.

Even though your boss acts like a mother, she is not your parent. Neither is she stupid or inept, just because she is nurturing. Thus, you will defeat your purpose and compromize your professionalism if you act like a child asking for a favour. When a young person deals with a parent, frustration is often the predominant emotion. If it is yours in this situation, keep it under control, no matter how the conversation is going. Stay calm and centred. Remember that you are a capable adult and a professional. Maintain your sense of self.

Show your respect, without going overboard; keep things businesslike and on track. Above all, meet her needs by including her in your plans, demonstrating concern for her during the discussion, and appealing to her desire for pleasant relationships and your need for her support.

Case study: customizing the steps

Clarify the benefits

Benefits answer the question: "What's in it for me?" or "How will this meet my needs?" In other words, why should your boss support your proposal? Here are some of the reasons you might present:

- Sales and Marketing should be working together more collaboratively in order to benefit the organization. By supporting this plan, she will be helping to bring that about.
- Others on her team feel as you do and will greatly appreciate her efforts on behalf of the proposal. She will be viewed as a team player for helping to further the team's goals.
- This will be good for the company, for her people, for the two departments involved, and for the customers. With her help, everyone will come out a winner.
- Management will praise her group (not her, as an individual, but her team).

Have the other person tell you what he or she will gain

Gently encourage your boss to tell you why this is a good thing to do and how everyone will be better off. She will probably not talk about herself, but about the department. Another kind of boss might assume credit for the idea; she will simply bask in her team's creativity and success.

If you've stated the benefits convincingly, and she gets your message, her response should be her own version of those same benefits. For example, she should agree that:

- The company will benefit from the improved collaboration between your department and Sales.
- She will reap the approval, respect, and admiration of her own team by helping it achieve its objectives.
- Her department will probably be singled out by management for praise and possibly reward for its innovative thinking and willingness to work together.

Tailor feedback for receptivity and effectiveness

Many interactions with people at work involve giving feedback of some kind, which is a learned skill. There are three ways to tailor it appropriately.

Individualized – tailored to the person
- Feedback should be specific.
- Address the behaviour, actions, or attitude of only that person.

Specific – tailored to an action or behaviour
- Direct criticism or praise toward a specific behaviour or activity.
- Focus on specifics and not personalities.

Timely – tailored to the appropriate moment.
- If possible, give feedback close to the event or behaviour.
- Don't wait until the next performance review to deliver it.

Feedback is necessary when:
- someone requests it
- unresolved problems persist
- errors occur repeatedly
- an employee's performance doesn't meet expectations
- a peer or your boss's work habits disturb you
- during performance reviews and appraisals
- during informal meetings, as appropriate

Getting feedback

Receiving feedback from others is not a passive process. Keep these questions in mind when receiving feedback.
- Am I willing to learn about other people, places and things?
- Would I want to know my boss's opinion of my listening ability?
- Do I listen for the main ideas the other person is trying to make?
- Do I try hard not to interrupt, even when I have something important or timely to add?
- Do I control any impulse to complete the other person's sentences?
- Do I tune in to the speaker's feelings, as well as to their words?
- Do I try to get beyond my own judgmental attitudes?

6

Know your options
Know your rights
Choose your response
Conclusion

**What more can I do?
Can I get out?
Can anyone help?**

What are your options?

There may come a point when you feel you have exhausted all of the techniques and ideas at your disposal and are feeling pretty desperate. Then what? Are you really out of options? The answer is no. Whatever your situation, there is always another alternative – always.

What if the tools and skills covered in the previous chapters do not work? You've read every book, tried every technique, gone for counselling, practiced assertiveness, bitten your tongue – and all for naught. You still have a boss, co-worker or subordinate who you cannot get along with; you are still stressed. Do you have any more options? What are they? Essentially you can:

■ accept and adjust
■ change something
■ leave

How will you choose your response?

Consider who might tend toward each of these options, based on their needs and behaviour.

■ Accept and adjust

The person most likely to adopt this option is REACTIVE (PASSIVE) + NO CONCERN FOR PEOPLE. They don't like to make waves or call attention to themselves, and are likely to take the line of least resistance, just cave in and suffer in silence; they certainly won't be active or storm out.

■ Change something

The person who will go all out to change something is PROACTIVE (DECISIVE) + PEOPLE ORIENTED.

LAST-RESORT OPTIONS

■ Grin and bear it.
■ Give up, and "retire on the job".
■ Seek help for yourself (higher up the chain of command).
■ Seek help for this person.
■ Try to have the person fired.
■ Look for another position within the company.
■ File a grievance.
■ Take legal action.
■ Leave the company.
■ Go public.

They will accept the challenge and try all possibilities. They will be willing to talk it through, state their case assertively, listen to the other side. This person will not cave in or give up until all options have been exhausted. Only then will they consider leaving.

■ Leave

The person most apt to pack their bags and hit the road is PROACTIVE (CONTROLLING) + NO CONCERN FOR PEOPLE . If they can't play by their rules, they will refuse to play. They will fight or switch, whichever gets the best results; but won't hang around and take a subservient position.

Accept and adjust

You may feel so trapped by circumstances that you seem to have no options, or so worn down by problems with your difficult boss or co-worker that you haven't got the emotional resources to remedy the situation. If so, you may feel that all you can do is grin and bear it or give up.

Grin and bear it

If you could grin and bear it, you probably would be doing that right now. Since you have not succeeded so far, chances are you won't get better with time.

However, if you can somehow alter your own way of seeing the situation and manage to simply tolerate the way things are, the upsides of this option are that you get to keep your job; you don't have to take the risks associated with some of the other suggested methods; you may get sympathy from others who know what you're going through; and you won't make waves.

However this will be at a price. The downsides include the wear and tear on your physical and emotional well-being; your diminished self-esteem for being a "doormat;" the loss of your productivity and creativity to the organization; and the sheer dishonesty of pretending everything is all right when it is anything but.

If your argument is that you can't afford to lose this job, that is valid but still a weak reason for selling out.

While you don't – or should not – leave your integrity and self-worth at the door when you come to work, grinning and bearing it is a viable option. You may find, though, that it is not a permanent one. You can only accept and adjust to a bad situation or the behaviour of a difficult person for so long before you are almost forced to move on and take another course of action   change something.

Give up, and retire on the job

Giving up and "retiring on the job" is definitely another way out; but, eventually someone is bound to notice that you are present in body only. When you stop performing, management can build a strong case for terminating you for non-performance. The good news is that perhaps nobody will notice what you're not doing for some time, and you can use that time to plan your future and take steps toward implementing the plan. The bad news, once again, is your overactive conscience, telling you it isn't right be paid when you haven't really earned it.

This option is a temporary measure, giving you chance to get your work life in order. It is not a permanent solution.

Change something

What can you change? Your own attitude, your approach to the other person, your physical location, your job, your company. Your own attitude is the one over which you have the most control.

You may have got to the end of the line as far as trying to reach an amicable solution to a difficult working relationship, but this doesn't mean that there is nothing else that you can do to change the situation.

Seek help for the other person

If you decide that the underlying reason for the difficult working relationship lies with the other person, and that they may need some kind of help, you might decide to take formal steps to get help for them.

If the person is a subordinate or co-worker, your first stop might be your immediate supervisor. In either case, this would be a matter of mutual concern; and together you could find the right help and persuade the person to take advantage of it.

If the person is your boss, you could go to Human Resources, or up the chain of command – in all cases, stressing that your motivation is concern, not vindictiveness or personal grievance. The Human Resources staff will be knowledgeable about available assistance. If necessary they will have the clout to compel your boss to get help or, at the very least, the influence to get someone in authority to do so.

Go up the chain of command

It may feel risky to go up the ladder for help, but sometimes it's a very useful tactic. If you are completely at a loss, your boss is the correct first stop. If she's a good manager, she will give you a fresh perspective or take things into her own hands. Even if you are a manager and are having trouble with one of your team, your boss can be of help, calling upon her own experience to advise you. You may also choose to go to some other manager with whom you have a good relationship. Your purpose is not to pass the buck up the line but to seek counsel from someone who has been in the trenches longer than you have.

Repercussions

If the cause of your misery is your boss, you could, of course, confront him, which could be difficult and risky and possibly backfire. You could go to his boss, but that person may not speak to you unless you have everything in writing and have already talked to your boss. This is definitely a "Catch 22", not to mention risky.

You may fear repercussion if you go over your boss's head, especially if you have a serious complaint about their behaviour, such as harassment or theft. You may suspect that whatever action you take will be used against you, and, unfortunately, it might. In some companies, if an employee's supervisor doesn't handle the situation satisfactorily, that person has a right to go to Human Resources or a higher authority. This is not universal practice and, even if it were, such a policy would be difficult to enforce and would not altogether alleviate your fears.

How can your boss get even with you for going over his or her head, without being obvious? You can be pretty sure she isn't going to fire you, but it is the subtle things that are harder to substantiate. For example, she could increase your workload, make unrealistic demands on your time, or give you responsibilities that are clearly beyond your scope – in other words, set you up to fail.

Share your problem

However, if you have faith in management, it is important that you do go up the chain of command. Chances are slim to none that top management has any idea about what is going on. The only way it is ever going to know is if someone goes out on a limb, overcomes their fear and tells them. Once you do it, you'll feel like the weight of the world has been lifted off your shoulders. Sometimes that alone is worth the risk.

Change something

There are four possible ways to change something: remove the source of the problem; file a grievance; take legal action; or go public. Each of them has its own pros and cons.

Try to get the person fired

If you wanted to have your nemesis fired, how would you go about it? If this person is a subordinate, it shouldn't be too difficult. If you covertly sabotage him or her by making unreasonable requests, piling on the work, and documenting every infraction, you might even survive a law suit. If the person is a peer, you could try a smear campaign through the grapevine, take advantage of every opportunity to badmouth him to your boss or anyone who will listen, or make sure others in authority are around to witness his behaviour. If it's your boss, it will be tougher, but possible, depending on your determination. Going up the chain of command is one way; filing a grievance is another; going to Human Resources is a third.

In other words, it can be done, but do you really want to go along that route? If you succeed, even though there may be compelling reasons why this person should be fired, do you want someone else's termination on your conscience?

Having someone fired is a serious matter, especially if the problem could have been resolved in another, more constructive way. Consider some of the other options before you end up resorting to this one.

File a grievance

Most companies do have formal grievance procedures. If yours does, find out from Human Resources what it is and how it works.

Some companies take an informal approach; others do it by the book. Generally, the steps are straightforward, but there is no question that this will not be an easy process for you. Knowing it will be difficult, it only makes good sense to educate yourself; weigh up the benefits and possible consequences; and be sure you have a knowledgeable, sympathetic person in your corner.

Some companies have formal policies. If someone has an allegation of sexual harassment, for example, the manager must go to Human Resources and report it. Once a formal complaint is lodged, Human Resources must go through the official procedure. Grievances are usually associated with union membership. A union member would file a formal grievance and go through a prescribed series of steps laid out in the union contract.

A grievance against a peer or boss that is found to be legitimate could lead to that person's discharge. While that is a serious consequence, if the other person's actions were serious enough to warant this, your action was justified.

Take legal action

If you have exhausted all other channels, don't have management support and can't find another job or afford to quit this one, then as a last resort, taking legal action may be the only option left to you.

Weigh it carefully. Only consider legal action if you are in an unbearable situation – one in which you are the object of excessive harassment or discrimination.

Suing the person who is making your life miserable, or suing your employer, is a complex activity with many unexpected pitfalls. For one thing, it's expensive; and many of those expenses are not apparent at first. The losing party is usually responsible for fees and court costs.

Getting embroiled in a law suit is also time consuming, often requiring many hours of paperwork, meetings, preparation for the case and time in court, if you get that far. The whole process is very stressful.

Even if you win, life could be tough for you if you choose to remain or return to your job when the suit is settled. If you lose, you will not have the option of returning; you may have spent a great deal of money with nothing to show for it. You must ask yourself "Am I willing to risk all that?"

Go public

If you have filed a grievance and that hasn't worked, you may choose to "go public." Don't even consider doing that unless your can back up every word you say with facts.

Going public may mean whistle-blowing or exposing your boss or co-worker to the media, the authorities, or the appropriate government agency. This is going to be time consuming, expensive, and stressful.

"Blowing the whistle" publicly is an absolute last resort and should only be considered in a very serious situation, such as unethical or illegal behaviour.

Document, document, document

Whatever action you decide on, do your homework before you act. Keep a detailed journal of what is going on and exactly what is said, by whom, and under what circumstances. If possible, tape your interactions so that you can quote verbatim.

Put everything you do or say in writing, and date it. Keep a copy of everything you write, including memos, e-mails, notes, letters, and performance reviews.

Ask other reliable witnesses to corroborate the incidents you are going to cite; if possible, get it in writing with their signatures.

Leave

Getting out of the environment that is causing you problems is a good idea. More and more companies are posting open positions so that present employees have first crack at them.

If you have the patience to wait for a suitable opening, this could be a good move for you. Sometimes, it's your only way out if your dealings with the difficult person are based solely on a clash of personalities. Of course, if you leave, you may be leaving the problem for your successor to deal with.

If you want to stay with your present company, you may be forced to make a change or take a detour in your career path. If you are willing to move to a whole different area – depending on the size and scope of your company's operations – such a move could open up opportunities for professional development you had not considered. Changing positions while staying with the same company demonstrates growth, gives you longevity and causes no disruption in your benefits or retirement programme. It could be the best thing you ever did.

Leave the company

Every professional should have an updated CV at all times. You never know when that one incident is going to put you over the edge, and make you decide it is time to start looking for another job.

One of the problems with job hunting is that you have to be prepared to tell potential employers why you want to leave your present position. Although you don't have to tell the whole truth and nothing but the truth, you're better off telling some of the truth without describing the whole of your nightmare experience. It is all right to say something along the lines of, "I don't think the career path I want to take is available to me in my current position." That's not a lie. When the interviewer asks for more information, only you can determine how specific you want to be.

The interviewer is not interested in hearing the details of your personal conflicts with a co-worker or your boss. But she may be interested in hearing about the positive way in which you handled a difficult situation.

TO LEAVE OR NOT TO LEAVE

Sometimes it is easier to make a decision between two opposite courses of action by simply comparing the advantages and disadvantages of each. Here is a review:

ADVANTAGES OF LEAVING

- Removing yourself from a problematic environment
- An opportunity for advancement elsewhere in the organization
- An opportunity to move to another geographic location
- Keeping your integrity intact
- Gaining the respect of your peers
- A new beginning

DISADVANTAGES OF LEAVING

- Fear of the unknown
- A possible detour in your career path
- The need to make a move to another geographic location
- Feeling like a quitter
- Losing the respect of your peers

Conclusion

As long as you work with other people, you are bound to find some of them difficult. While this book has provided you with many valuable tools to help you deal with them, the single most important tool at your disposal is your own ability to choose how you will respond to any person or situation.

Difficult people are a part of life – inevitable, inescapable, unfathomable. Even with an entire book of practical advice on how to survive working with them, you may still be asking yourself, "Why do they behave that way?" There are as many answers to that question as there are difficult people; but, to refresh your memory, go back and reread Chapter One. Sometimes, if you understand the why of behaviour, the how becomes just a little bit easier.

This book begins with that very subject by asking, "What is a difficult person, and why does he or she act that way?" The reasons are rarely obvious unless the person is willing to share that information with you. Chapter One covers some possible reasons. There are many more, of course; but the point is that we do not usually know what is beneath the surface. All we have to deal with is the behaviour itself.

Chapter Two provides the immediate attitudes and actions that will diffuse a potentially volatile situation. The first is simply to remember that this is not your problem. The others are much easier: stay centred; choose your response; ask questions; be assertive; negotiate; let them vent; remember

conflict resolution; and if you are still getting nowhere fast, call time out.

What you should not do in the heat of battle is every bit as important as what you should do. Avoid doing all the wrong things and at least you won't make the situation any worse. If you follow the advice in Chapters Two and Three and keep things on an even keel, the more sophisticated techniques in later chapters will be more effective.

The heart of this book is the ten-step format. The steps are just good common sense, but it is amazing how many people have never think of approaching an argument in this way. Try it and see how well it works.

The ten steps will work just as they are presented in Chapter Four, but the ability to tailor them to a specific person's needs gives you an advantage few people have. If you understand the concept of matching needs to behaviour, you can deal with virtually any person and situation.

No one likes to admit failure, but it is unrealistic to think it will never occur. The last chapter deals with that very possibility: what to try when you've tried everything. You can accept and adjust; you can change something; or you can leave.

Index

abuse, verbal, 30
accept and adjust, 86, 87
action plan, 57
aggression, 34
agreement, 41, 50, 54
apologizing, 43
assertiveness, 22, 23, 73
behaviour, 12, 13, 65, 80, 86
bosses, 66–71
building a bridge, 54, 55
centredness, 16
changing things, 86, 88
cognitive style, 12
common ground, 26
communicating, 66
conflict resolution, 26, 27
conflict, handling, 38
confronting issues, 72

criticism, 21
delegating, 66
detachment, 42, 43
documenting events, 91
ego, 34, 39
emotion, 25, 32, 35
empathy, 47
employees, 74–77
extenuating circumstances, 56
feedback, 26, 53, 83
follow through, 58
grievance procedure, 90
help, seeking, 88
last-resort options, 86
leaving, 42, 86, 92–3
legal action, 91
listening, 34, 52
Maslow's hierarchy of needs, 62

mediator, 26
meeting, calling a, 48
meetings, 78–79
Myers-Briggs Type Indicator, 12
needs, 24, 65, 81, 86
negotiation, 24
options, 86
peers, 72–73
personality types, 12
personalizing issues, 16, 73
persuasion, 20
planning, 48
positive self-talk, 16
proactivity, 13, 16, 17
questions, 20, 52
reacting, 42
reactivity, 13, 16, 17
reflecting, 53

resolving differences, 56, 57
respect, 47, 66
responding, 42, 81
response, 18, 23, 34, 86
retaliation, 32
"ritual opposition", 40
space needs, 39
stating your position, 55
summarizing, 53
teamwork, 66
telephone communication, 78
ten-step format, 46
time out, 27, 35
truth, 41
understanding, 20
venting, 25, 26
violence, 36, 37
"win: win" outcomes, 24, 47, 56